Timeless Lessons

A Psychotherapist's Journey and Insights for His Family

BY
MANNIE SHER

With a Foreword
by
Olya Khaleelee

MAPLE
PUBLISHERS

Timeless Lessons

Author: Mannie Sher

Copyright © 2024 Mannie Sher

The right of Mannie Sher to be identified as author of this work has been asserted by the author in accordance with section 77 and 78 of the Copyright, Designs and Patents Act 1988.

First Published in 2024

ISBN 978-1-83538-344-5 (Paperback)
     978-1-83538-345-2 (Hardback)
     978-1-83538-346-9 (E-Book)

Book cover design and Book layout by:
    White Magic Studios
    www.whitemagicstudios.co.uk

Published by:
    Maple Publishers
    Fairbourne Drive, Atterbury,
    Milton Keynes,
    MK10 9RG, UK
    www.maplepublishers.com

A CIP catalogue record for this title is available from the British Library.

All rights reserved. No part of this book may be reproduced or translated in any form or by any means, electronic or mechanical, including photocopying, recording or by any information storage and retrieval system without written permission from the author.

This book is a memoir. It reflects the author's recollections of experiences over time. Some names and characteristics have been changed, some events have been compressed, and some dialogues have been recreated, and the Publisher hereby disclaims any responsibility for them.

Dedication

To my beloved Leonie,

My partner in life, my source of strength, and my truest friend.

Your unwavering love, wisdom, and resilience have been my constant guide.

This memoir is as much yours as it is mine, for none of it would have been possible without you by my side.

Thank you.

Contents

Dedication 3

Acknowledgements 7

Olya Khaleelee 9

Introduction 11

Letter # 1 – Why A Memoir? 14

Letter # 2 – The Biology of Our Senses 19

Section # 1 – My Early Years, Illness and Dissolution of my Family

Letter # 3 – My Parents, Religion and Later Professional Life 22

Letter # 4 – Asthma (1944 to 1947) 27

Letter # 5 – Letter to my sister, Goldie 30

Section # 2 – Adulthood, Restoration of my Family, and Moving from South Africa to Great Britain

Letter # 6 – Johannesburg (1953) 33

Letter # 7 – Religion - Wrong-headed thinking leading to bad things happening 35

Letter # 8 – Passover 37

Letter # 9 – Parenting (1960s and 1970s) 39

Letter # 10 – Leonie, Our Children and Our Arrival in London (August 1967) 41

Letter # 11 – Mixed feelings about Separation and Christian National Education 47

Section # 3 – My Professional Journey - Social Work, Psychiatric Social Work, Psychotherapy & Organisational Consultancy

Letter # 12 – Mary Barker (1971 to 1987) 51

Letter # 13 – Dorothea Brande on *Becoming a Writer* 56

Letter # 14 – Writing 58
Letter # 15 – Writing 61
Letter # 16 – On Writing 63

Section # 4 – My Psychoanalytic Treatment
Letter # 17 – The First Dream 67
Letter # 18 – A Dream 70
Letter # 19 – A Dream 74
Letter # 20 – A Dream 77

Section # 5 – Societal Challenges
Letter # 21 – Society 82
Letter # 22 – Kibbutz (1958) – An Experiment in Social Living 84
Letter # 23 – Politics (1960s – 1970s) 87
Letter # 24 – Two Films 93
Letter # 25 – Private Medical Insurance 98
Letter # 26 – Sex 104
Letter # 27 – Wrong-headedness in International Relations 107

Section # 6 – My Senior Years
Letter # 28 – Kidney failure and dialysis 112
Letter # 29 – Kidney Dialysis 118
Letter # 30 – Kidney Dialysis 125

Section # 7 – Letters to my Children
Letter # 31 – Thoughtful Concentration and Taking In 134
Letter # 32 – Educating our Children for the Spiritual Life 137
Letter # 33 – Collapse 140
Letter # 34 – Twin Grandchildren 143

Letter # 35 – Second Child 145
Letter # 36 – Humour 149
Letter # 37 – Restoration, Despair and Optimism 152
Letter # 38 – Family Visits – Judaism & Psychoanalysis 159
Letter # 39 – Various – Writing, Psychoanalysis & Dream..................165

Section # 8 – Letters to my Grandchildren
Letter # 40 – Athletics – Matar 171
Letter # 41 – Not Losing (Athletics) 177
Letter # 42 – Desire – Adeena 179
Letter # 43 – The Love of Sharing..182
Letter # 44 – The Conflict between Self-interest and Loyalty to Others 185
Letter # 45 – Allergies 189
Letter # 46 – The Religious Life..192
Letter # 47 – Art...195
Letter # 48 – A Letter to the Twins, Shiloh & Lily..................................197
Letter # 49 – Nadav – Officer in the IDF and the Middle East War...........200
Letter # 50 – Integration of Cultures..202
Letter # 51 – Work Groups 204
Letter # 52 – The Youngest Child..208
Letter # 53 – Adeena's Birthday...210
Letter # 54 – The Israel-Gaza War and Anti-Semitism 214
Letter # 55 – The Impact of Kidney Dialysis on Me 216
Letter # 56 – Decisions Made and Unmade...220
Letter # 57 – A Letter to Leonie...224
Conclusion..227
A testimonial from Adeena Sher, Granddaughter 230

Acknowledgements

This book is the culmination of many years of work, and I could not have completed it without the unwavering love and support of my dearest Leonie. Your editorial guidance, thoughtful advice, and endless encouragement have been vital throughout this journey. Over the decades, you have been my anchor, my partner, and my greatest source of strength. Your belief in me and this project helped bring it to life, and for that, I am profoundly grateful.

A special thanks to my sister, Goldie, for our weekly chats. Your recollections helped fill in many gaps in my memory and brought to life forgotten parts of our family's history. Your contributions added depth and richness to the stories I've shared here.

I would also like to thank Jacqueline Burns, author, and Founder of the London Writer's Club, whose insight and leadership inspired me to turn a long-held dream into reality. The members of the 2022-23 Masterclass offered a unique blend of camaraderie and motivation, helping a group of passionate amateur writers find the courage to craft and complete their books.

My heartfelt thanks go to Ed Craft of Wedlake Bell LLP for his perceptive comments and wise advice, which have been of great value.

Finally, my deepest gratitude goes to my children—Shanan, Yoram, and Danny—and to my grandchildren. Though none of you asked to be written about, you welcomed the final result with love and understanding, offering me the space to reflect and share our family's journey.

Shanan, your quiet wisdom and grace have been a guiding light throughout my life. Yoram, your strength, resilience, and determination remind me of the importance of perseverance even in the face of adversity. Danny, your humour, warmth, and open-heartedness have been a constant source of joy, especially during the most difficult moments.

And to my grandchildren: your presence in my life has given me a new perspective on legacy and the future. Each of you carries forward the values that Leonie and I have tried to instil—love, kindness, and a sense of belonging. Your curiosity, energy, and individuality have inspired me to see the world through fresh eyes. As I wrote this book, I often thought of the future you are shaping, and I hope that in some small way, this work reflects the love and guidance I've tried to pass on to you.

The legacy we have built together as a family is not just reflected in this book but in the lives you, my children and grandchildren, lead every day. This book is a testament to the bonds we share, the lessons we've learned, and the values we hold dear. It is our story as much as it is mine—rooted in resilience, love, and mutual respect.

Your patience and understanding as I explored our family history and shared personal reflections have been invaluable. Writing about those we love can be a delicate task, and yet each of you—my children and grandchildren—has shown great compassion, offering me the freedom to express my truths. My letters to you were not crafted by design, but by the soft pull of whoever lived most vividly in my thoughts as I wrote. Yet I hold the hope that these words, though addressed to one cherished soul, may still speak to all hearts that know the language of longing and love.

Our legacy lives on through you. It fills me with immense pride to see how our family's journey continues to grow and thrive with each new generation. The love we have nurtured together transcends the pages of this book and will continue to shape the lives of our descendants. Thank you for being part of this journey, for embracing my words, and for allowing me to reflect on the rich and meaningful legacy we share.

Foreword

Olya Khaleelee

Written at a time when liberal democracy – indeed the entire world order - is under fire, this autobiography attests to the resilience and strength of the human spirit. Mannie Sher has produced a moving and fascinating memoir linking his individual experience with the social and political context in which he has lived. His memoir takes the form of personal letters and postcards to his children and grandchildren, thereby creating a link not only between the generations but within the historical developments of our time. Each communication is a vignette embodying Mannie's personal experience and linking them with his ideas and his teachings, thereby, in each case, transmitting something new. Whilst his audience is his children and grandchildren "in the mind", these published reflections provide much food for thought and learning for the reader. Through his personal psychoanalysis, his clinical practice and his many years' experience working in the field of group relations and through consulting to organisations at the Tavistock Institute of Human Relations, Mannie imparts to the reader the true value of learning by experience. He communicates the importance of creating the context for learning – creating the boundary conditions - as the key to enabling change at both conscious and unconscious levels, rather than the belief that teaching someone enables that individual to change in their inner world. The change process needs to come from within that individual, driven by inner self-empowerment, rather than coming from an external source, although having an external resource, such as therapeutic help, is clearly supportive for the process.

Each letter is addressed personally to his three sons and to each of his grandchildren, additionally with a wider audience in mind. The title of this book. "*Timeless Lessons*" was chosen because Mannie wanted to keep in mind "real people with real issues and conflicts who were moving into their 'futures'" while acknowledging, now that he is in his eighties and in poor health, that his own life is coming to an end.

His aim is: "to inspire the reader to be in touch with their own inner experiences of memories, emotions, and feelings, hopes and desires and fulfilment through the joys of living." There is no doubt that through this fascinating, engaging, and moving memoir, he has achieved his goal. I encourage the reader to take the journey with Mannie Sher through his Timeless Lessons.

Olya Khaleelee

Corporate Psychologist

Chairwoman, OPUS: Organisation for Promoting Understanding of Society.

Introduction

The Russian invasion of Ukraine in February 2022 brought the world as we know it, to an end. Human freedoms, the rights of free expression and movement, and the trust we place in our elected representatives, already weakened over the previous decade, were all upended. We can no longer take liberal democracy for granted or rely on the hope that tinpot tyrants and dictators will turn reasonable and offer their subjugated people democratic institutions and support the rights of the individual under law. Instead, we now realise that however liberal, kind, caring and compassionate we and our Western society might be, a democratic way of life needs to be protected and defended, by taking up arms, if necessary, against the destructive bullies whose main objective is to remain in power, and subjugate everyone and all institutions that challenge them.

Is it only "them" that are guilty of this destructiveness? Or are we complicit, and compromised by our wilful blindness to see what is happening, colluding with autocrats because their energy sources are cheap and easily available? Have we become smug and complacent in our standards of living, and narcissistic preoccupations with selfish desires? In pointing fingers at the destructiveness of others, are we denying our own tendencies towards self-destructiveness?

I did not set out to write a book about international conflict, even though I believe there is a straight line between individual experience and social and political behaviour. I intended to write a book, *Timeless Lessons*, to members of my family about the mind and the consequences of wrong-headed thinking in our individual stories, in my family's narratives and in social and national myths and legends. But that is a huge task and for me in my early 80s, time is short; so, I decided to write a personal memoir in the form of 'Letters' to my children, grandchildren, and their descendants. In this way, I had hoped to create a bridge between the past, the present and something new so that the reader would be able to link themselves to history and see themselves as carrying a tradition of critical thought into their own age and onwards to their descendants.

Timeless Lessons consists of a series of vignettes of my experiences and feelings I have in the moment of writing. The vignettes are short enough to be read quickly, contain stimulating ideas and offer the potential for learning something new. The vignettes are personal and include clinical case studies and dream interpretation, which were chosen because they contain 'lessons-for-life' for a generation that is searching for meaning in the midst of, at times, an incomprehensible world, a world that is moving at a rapid pace and which confuses and bewilders, which is sometimes nasty and disappointing, and only patchily nurturing and developmental; a world that increasingly requires people to create their own opportunities for contentment and satisfaction.

I would not want the 'lessons-for-life' idea to be cast in stone, or a ritualised set form of words, but rather to be seen as provocations for thinking new thoughts, and stimuli for deeper personal reflection. Thoughts may lie buried deep in the mind and may need a trigger to float them to the surface, where they can be accessed consciously and become an important part of the individual's 'self' and their way of relating to others.

The vignettes in *Timeless Lessons* are selected randomly from the masses of thoughts I experience. They are arranged in sections from my early years to the autumn years of my life. Usually, I have little idea where the thoughts might end up. I am intrigued by the mysteries of the mind, and I aim for my writing to have a sensible coherent structure and for the book to have an interesting and relevant title. My children and grandchildren are my 'audience-in-the-mind', and I strive to address what I think are their concerns and questions.

I hope the mini-essays have appeal to a general readership too, especially to younger and older people who are concerned about the continuity of life, who are hopeful about the future, respecters of tradition and values, without withdrawing from modernity and the urgency to participate in social and personal obligations in the service of others and in promoting social change. This book will interest people who consider themselves to be philosophical, who are able to be thoughtful in the face of a setback, or who can approach a tough situation in a level-headed way and with resilience. We could call them conscientious thinkers. I have endeavoured to put down on paper in straightforward language, seemingly complex ideas. I did not set out to complicate things more than they are, but to inspire the reader to be in touch with their own inner experiences of memories, emotions, and feelings, hopes and desires and fulfilment through the joys of living.

Letter #1

Why A Memoir?

3rd August 2021

Dear Shanan, Yoram and Danny

Covid is upon us, I am in my 80s, and I think the time has come to share my reflections with you on issues connected with my life, the choices I have made, and to familiarise you with people and events, choices, and decisions which you may have only vaguely known about. We are an immigrant family, removed from our roots in South Africa. The cycle gets repeated and you, Shanan and Danny, are separated from us by distance in Israel, as Mum and I once moved away from our parents to Great Britain, and increased their isolation and sadness by taking you, *their* grandchildren, with us.

By emigrating from South Africa, I have been fortunate in having had opportunities in my professional life that I doubt I would have had in South Africa. I have had an interesting life and achieved many things I had wanted to achieve. But I am not different from thousands of others who have also had interesting or troubled lives from whom one could learn much. I like teaching, imparting knowledge that is helpful to people, but I am careful not to impose that knowledge. Through my own personal psychoanalysis and working at the Tavistock Clinic in the 1970s and the Tavistock Institute, from 1997 to the present time, that included deep association with Group Relations Conference work, I have become imbued with the philosophy of learning from and through experience. Conveying knowledge from one brain to another is a delicate process that must be approached with humility, caution, and sensitivity. Whether in psychotherapy with patients (individual, couples, or groups) or with clients in research and consultation (with organisations, communities, and the wider society), ambivalence in the form of a desire for knowledge coupled with a resistance to acquiring it, needs to be recognised. As a consultant, I claim the possibility of benefiting from my knowledge, but I also know that my interventions do not produce results; it is the patient, or the client, who goes away and produces results elsewhere, perhaps after absorbing some of my views about their situations, but the results always belong to the patient or client, never to me. My role is to provide a containing, safe space for the patient or client to voice their hopes and fears, their plans, and reviews of their plans, and to help them gather new perspectives. My job is to question existing beliefs and help create new beliefs that are more adapted to the changes occurring in individuals and in their social environments. This is the complete antithesis of the faith paradigm which is to retain belief in stories, legends and principles which cannot (or ought not to) be questioned, whereas the basis of modern science, and I regard myself as a scientist, is to test hypotheses to destruction. Illusions rather than reality are often preferred; unpredictability and uncertainty cannot be tolerated easily and are dealt with by turning stories into concrete realities. In my work, I share interpretations of what I am hearing from patients or clients relative to their inner world phantasies, ideas and feelings that are mostly external to their conscious awareness and cannot easily be put into words. If done carefully, slowly, and repeatedly, and in soft tones, and as part of a shared voyage involving commitment to a working relationship by both parties, minds begin to open to let in new thoughts – the beginning of change. I am committed to this type of learning, and I express this desire in my psychotherapy practice and in Group Relations, a method of experiential learning that was developed in the 1950s at the Tavistock Institute and Tavistock Clinic by pioneers who sought to extend psychoanalytic knowledge and processes outside the consulting room into social structures in wider society.

So, back to my question: why a memoir in the form of letters to you my children and grandchildren? I regard myself as an influencer and a producer, rather than a consumer. Aristotle claimed that human beings are political animals by nature, and this nature is acquired by living in a 'polis', in a city, i.e. by being in contact with others. I believe purpose and role in the polis give more meaning to life than simple togetherness and materialistic consumption. And I believe that everyone is capable to some degree of being an influencer or producer that helps satisfy the needs of others through increased awareness, insight, and empathy. I question the religious view that faith alone achieves this. One does not need faith to lead a good and ethical life. Ethical behaviour is moderate, it lies at the mean; it is socially constructed, and it does not need martyrs, saints, or heroes in extreme situations to inspire it. We are all accountable for our behaviour to live ethically, and to be able to demonstrate our reliability and to be continuously worthy within ourselves and socially.

In writing this memoir in the form of letters to you and my descendants, I hope you would understand that it is possible to make constructive and creative individual journeys despite family, educational and social pressures to conform to a particular way of thinking and being that comes from group affiliation or from society. It may be comforting to sink into the bosom of one's group, but it is a false security, because the 'group' as a group, has intentions of its own and it uses its members to fulfil those intentions, thus compromising their individuality. Always be sceptical of the silky words of leaders who sell you a line, anaesthetise your thoughts and emotions and invite you to support their versions of reality, not yours. Facilitation, not instruction; holding hands, not pushing, increases your chances of producing creative selves, and ethical cultures, based on care and compassion, without losing sight of the need to accomplish practical tasks. There is a fine line between integrity and profit, and it is possible to have both. My father taught me that satisfied customers are worth everything.

When I was thinking what to call this book, I thought of several possible titles like: "Don't Take your Dilemmas at Face Value. Dig Deeper!"; "Attend to what is outside of Awareness"; "Where do you Mostly Live? In the Past or the Future?" I finally settled on *"Timeless Lessons"* because I wanted to keep in my mind real people with real issues and conflicts who were moving into their 'futures' while mine was coming to an end.

When your children, my grandchildren, were troubled by something in their families or at school, or with friends, or wanted their dreams interpreted, they would call me and ask to have a 'private conversation'. I enjoy the 'kindly grandfather' role and in addition to the relief they get out of it, they also see the fun side, and I experience a profound joy of establishing a warm connection with them. I don't think they see me as old-fashioned; I am quite revolutionary and contemporary and aware that survival in work and in relationships in the 21st Century will come about through flexibility and adaptability, an ability to think new thoughts, not rigidity and orthodoxy; more relationship-oriented than rules-based.

I am putting my letters to you in the form of a book because I think it will interest other grandparents; building a bridge between generations and help to take you and my grandchildren from a familiar place to discover something new. My hope is that this book is educative, visionary, innovative and transformational. I have always wanted to transform lives with good ideas and help people let go of bad ones. Ideas is about language, and this was my problem – at school I was not particularly good at language, but later I learned of its value.

Early in my clinical practice I was treating an ultra-orthodox Jewish man for whom English was a second language. He had brought his 7-year-old son for treatment following the death of the family's 6-month-old infant. For months we worked together to help him understand his feelings about the tragedy that had resulted from his wrong-headed idea that was then current thinking in some families (and professionals), that babies should be left to cry until they fall asleep. The father described how he sat in the next room to the baby, the baby cried desperately for hours, and he did nothing to soothe it, believing that not attending to him was the right thing to do. The man's faith was important to him, and he relied on it to explain the death of his baby – he could not face or deal his feelings of guilt and sadness. He was not open to the possibility of insight, and he came to his sessions with me out of duty to his surviving children and his wife, not because of any felt need for 'repair' in himself. At the end of our time together, I asked what he thought he had gained from our sessions. He said he had not gained much understanding of the tragedy or how to help his son, but his English had improved! The language we speak changes our perception of the world and shapes our concepts. Language is used not only to communicate, but to express the 'self', to reach out and relate with others. My patient's world view was built on an unshakeable foundation, and perhaps he was offering me a 'gift' by saying that the improvement in his language had changed his world view and his understanding of his family, but he could not easily acknowledge that.

Your loving Dad, Mannie

Letter #2

The Biology of Our Senses

17ᵗʰ August 2021

Dear Shanan, Yoram and Danny

I hope this finds you well amidst the demands of your osteopathic clinics, Shanan and Danny, and the whirlwind of your slow, high intensity rehabilitation gym, Yoram, my professional companions! I figured I'd drop you a note delving into the fascinating realm of our senses.

So, picture this: we navigate the world, unravel its mysteries, and dodge its pitfalls through a symphony of senses – sight, smell, hearing, touch, taste, and even that lesser-known sensation called proprioception, where our brain tells us where our body is in space. Oh, and let's not forget about interoception, our internal sensors providing us with intelligence on hunger, thirst, pain, and a whole spectrum of feelings.

Now, observing your own children, those little bundles of curiosity and chaos, you've likely marvelled at how they absorb the world – learning its ropes, embracing its delights, and side-stepping its hazards. It's like Freud's pain-pleasure principle takes the steering wheel, guiding their choices to dodge discomfort and snatch some joy.

Do you remember those early months of parenthood? Babies, with their basic survival mode engaged, focus on the essentials: sucking, swallowing, digesting, and, well, nappy-changing rituals. Growth, time, and routines become the architects of their developing nervous systems, fostering a sense of predictability and safety.

Sure, parenting isn't all smooth sailing – mistakes, delays, and a dash of chaos are par for the course. Yet, chronic experiences like maternal depression, family strife, or external upheavals can leave lasting imprints on a youngster's physical and psychological growth. Those early years set the stage for confidence or its absence, shaping relationships with friends, partners, and even authority figures down the line.

As our little ones grow, the influences broaden – from family dynamics to the sway of teachers, friends, and the omnipresent social media. The home's impact remains potent, but the day will come when it competes with external forces.

Babies and toddlers, in their perpetual learning mode, become mini-detectives, scanning their mom's face for emotional cues. They're all about routines – hunger, feeding, contentment, pooping, nappy changing, and snoozing – building the foundations of a lifetime.

Fun fact: those tiny nervous systems aren't fully cooked at birth, taking around eight weeks to kick into gear. Myelin, the magic insulating layer around nerves, starts doing its thing. Before this, it's all about survival instincts – breathing, sucking, digesting – with the caregiver, usually Mom, playing the superhero role. This dynamic duo sets the stage for a lifetime of love, care, loyalty, and continuity.

Now, let's not forget the brain and nervous system's ongoing development until around the age of 25. A newborn's twitchy, jerky movements smooth out as the nervous system matures, thanks to soothing routines and a bit of bedtime magic. Responding to cries with patience and avoiding irritation and hostility – it's like baby zen mode.

So, here's to the incredible journey of sensory exploration and growth! Until next time.

Cheers,

Your loving Dad

Section 1

My Early Years, Illness and Dissolution of my Family

Letter #3

My Parents, Religion and Later Professional Life

17th October 2021

Dear Shanan, Yoram & Danny

A child stares out of the window of the train at the passing South African Highveld as he ponders what his future holds, probably feeling sad about the family he has just left behind. He cannot recollect ever having been asked whether he wanted to make this journey to a faraway place – a thousand miles hence to live with a different family for reasons that were not clear to him, except that "it would be best for his health". Perhaps he was excited - train journeys always are - the clickety clack of the wheels as the train snaked its way up from the coast to the hinterland - and sleeping two nights on bunks on the train - pure joy, wrapped in South African Railways crisp white sheets and blue blankets with the emblematic SAR initials woven into the fabric, and the mixed race men who came towards evening to make the bunks up, while the boy and his mother ate their egg sandwiches with tea. At age 7, was the boy ready for this dislocation of his life - school, friends, and family? It seemed these considerations were not given a thought - there was a health problem, and moving from the damp and windy coast was deemed the solution - but whose problem was it? His? His mother's? His family's, at a point of crisis? On reflection, it dawns on him that there was a slow inexorable movement towards the dissolution of the family as it was known - with hindsight, it appears that the problem was, in part, the boy's mother's feelings of suffocation in the family. It was she who needed to escape the confines of the family, and gaining her freedom was the price I had to pay. Perhaps this is the reason the little boy felt suspicious of attempts to "help" him. "Being helped" seldom came without a price tag attached. He learned that "being helped" potentially enslaved him to the helper; it involved a loss of power and potency to the warm seductiveness of the helper, a sense of entrapment of which he learned to be watchful. This loss of power later inverted and became a source of great power for the boy who absorbed it and utilised it to consolidate his position in the affections of others - his mother, in the first instance, through tidying his bedroom and the rest of the house, making tea for his mother, and in adulthood, choosing a helping profession for the most disabled people in society. No problem was too big or insurmountable, except of course not recognizing that the biggest problem that needed attention, was himself, and the guilt that drove him, and was also slowly destroying him. It had prevented him from developing other talents and finding joy in other pursuits or attending to the needs of his own family. Being a "helping person" became part of his identity, which was mainly directed towards others, while his family was left contending with his anger, depression, irascibility, his despair, and negativity. How could the "helper" be so unhelpful towards his own family?

My father had a relaxed, but respectful, attitude towards Judaism and its traditions, but my mother believed in them with nary a critical thought. She had a closed mind of fixed ideas based on superstition and fear of a vengeful God's punishment and retribution, usually taking the form of illness, poverty, humiliation, reduced social status and the inheritance of hell. Once an idea took hold in my mother, for instance that for health reasons, I should move and live with my aunt and uncle, a thousand miles away, there was no swaying her from that idea, not even my father could. There was no consideration given to the impact this would have on my psychological development, only on perfecting the conditions of my physical health and my religious education. The only effect on my mother of my deeply troubled and unhappy experience with my new family, bullied and rejected, was to be unsympathetic and angry with me for spoiling her arrangements. It felt to me that she could not be bothered with me as I was an irritant and a nuisance and she wanted her freedom from a wilful, whingeing, wheezing and sick child. The fact that my sister, Goldie, was also sent away to boarding school, leaving my mother free of parenting responsibilities to travel abroad for lengthy periods, confirmed for me that my mother's selfishness and fear of social criticism were important elements in the culture of our family. And, of course, there was the guilt she must have felt, guilt that was presumably caused by abandoning her children to others, guilt because she must have known that she could not love. Stern observance of rules had replaced any compassion she may have felt towards her children. My psychoanalysis helped me to consider another angle – that my mother intuitively knew she was not a good mother, that she was emotionally impoverished, and that sending me away, possibly saved me from her stifling personality. Of course, the repressed pain of my difficult relationship with her re-surfaced during my long psychoanalysis, got repeatedly re-played in my relationship with my analyst, with mum and with you, my three growing children. As my insights grew, small gains were made in my ability to accept and to love members of my family and myself unconditionally, but it was never perfect; from time to time I would regress to the characteristics of my earlier primary relationship with my mother; going through the pain all over again and again, and relying on the loving acceptance of the people in my life, to come to my senses and recover some degree of maturity and responsibility. This realisation included that, however limited it was, my mother was as caring of me as she was able to be, probably mitigated by her unbearable suffering she was experiencing of looking after a child who could not breathe and whose life was continuously in her hands. In those days, there was little understanding of how family dynamics meant that the conditions of one member of the family could be identified with and resemble those of another member. Putting it another way, the difficulty of my breathing, with insight, could have been explained as a manifestation of my mother's constant efforts to keep me under her control so that neither she nor I could breathe freely – we were both locked in some mutually collusive struggle for oxygenated independence and autonomy, and our relationship ensured that neither of us had any – until she managed to separate us by sending me to her sister, a decision supported by the medical profession at whose feet she worshipped.

And so, it became thus in my clinical, consultancy and education and training work – struggling to adopt and maintain a reasoned, sensible criticalness in my thinking and a wider tolerance of mess and disorder than I had been able to do before. Curiously, in the 1970s and 1980s, in my career in group relations conference work, I came to see how groups are drawn persistently towards the messianic phantasy. When groups are at certain stages of tackling their tasks, they invariably conjure a phantasy that one of their number will step into a messianic role in the unfulfillable hope of solving the group's dilemmas by imposing order and taking the group from a place of chaos and threatened disintegration to a state of tranquillity and satisfaction. I am interested in the process that transforms a group phantasy into a dogma of the faith which I suspect connects to the size and length of existence of the group and the increasingly frightening threats of group violence, as seen in history in the removal of rights, persecution, totalitarianism, wars and annihilations, and the Holocaust, in the case of the Jews. Jews are no strangers to the contempt and murderousness of messianic religions; the newer religions seek their legitimacy not by what is good about them, but by the ways that differentiate them from the original religion. Judaism, a non-conversion religion, defined messianism as a state of being, a society based on justice for all within a political framework of independence and self-rule; the new religion claimed superiority through its bizarre dogmas of a perfect person conceived without a sperm somehow reaching an ovum that would lead to an absurd conflict-free paradise.

I sometimes wonder might my mother also have been aiming for her phantasised paradise through trying to get her child to breathe? Beyond the understanding of my relationship with my mother, my analysis provided several additional insights. I gained awareness of how family dynamics and unresolved issues can be passed down through generations. My mother's struggles with emotional expression and her rigid adherence to religious beliefs were, in part, responses to her own upbringing and the cultural context she was part of. Recognizing these patterns allowed me to break the cycle and approach my own parenting and relationships differently.

I developed a deeper understanding of the unconscious motivations driving my actions. My compulsion to help others and the associated guilt were revealed as attempts to compensate for feelings of inadequacy and unresolved childhood conflicts. This insight helped me recognize similar unconscious processes in others, enriching my professional work.

My analysis illuminated the dual nature of the helper role—how it can be both a source of strength and a trap. My desire to help others, while altruistic, was also a way to gain validation and avoid facing my own vulnerabilities. This awareness allowed me to redefine my approach to helping, focusing on genuine compassion rather than a need for control or approval.

The process taught me to tolerate ambiguity and imperfection, both in myself and others. Understanding that my mother's actions were influenced by her limitations allowed me to accept her flaws without resentment. This acceptance extended to my own imperfections, fostering a more compassionate and realistic view of my identity and capabilities.

Finally, my analysis helped me move toward emotional independence. By disentangling myself from the need for external validation and approval, I found a more authentic sense of self. This journey toward autonomy enabled me to pursue my interests and passions with greater clarity and less fear of judgment.

Overall, these insights contributed to a more integrated and compassionate understanding of myself, my family, and the world around me.

Your loving father, Mannie

Letter #4
Asthma (1944 to 1947)

29th October 2021

Dear Shanan, Yoram & Danny

In a recent conversation with my sister, older by five and a half years, we reminisced about our parents and our lives as young children 70 to 80 years ago in Port Elizabeth and reached the awful, but freeing conclusion that my mother was depressed, miserable and probably unhappy in her marriage to our father and in her role as a mother. It is also likely that my father's early deprivation, the murder of his family, and his escape from Lithuania to make a new life for himself in Palestine, had contributed to his sadness, short temper and intense frustration with my mother, whose expectations of the distinguished life of a white, Jewish madam he could barely fulfil. And besides he was not the original love of her life. She had previously been engaged but was forbidden to marry by her mother until all her other 8 children had married in the correct order. Her suitor decided he could not wait and left. Managing with second best was never one of my mother's strong points, and I think she bore a deep resentment for most of her life that her social ambitions had been thwarted, although in her later years, after my father suffered a heart attack, she mellowed, and showed she cared for my father deeply, suggesting that she did have a capacity to love after all, but perhaps I never felt it through her attempts at control.

The conversation with my sister, Goldie, turned to the asthma that I had suffered as a child, and which was the alleged reason for being sent to live with my mother's older sister at the age of seven. Goldie repeated the reason given for being sent away for health reasons - the windy Eastern Cape was no place for asthmatics. I remember the asthma well, the wheezing, the difficulty breathing, the fear of suffocating. I was desperate and I expect my parents were driven to distraction by me. I was taken from doctor to doctor all to no effect, until it was suggested that I should be moved to a dry climate. Like with all her relationships with rabbis and doctors, my mother was obsessively fawning and sycophantic towards them - 'yes, doctor, this, yes, doctor that'. Having several nephews as doctors who could be approached for advice, produced a cabal of authoritative medical men who were united in promoting their private views, often by intrigue and usually unknown to those who were affected by their views. 'Auntie needs placating', they said. They arrogantly claimed knowledge and understanding of relationships they had no right to, being stunted in their own growth, and maintained by their upwardly mobile social standing of white male doctors in a society structured according to race theories of superiority. They all agreed that sending me to the Transvaal would be the best thing for me. And so my mother handed the burden of caring for me and bringing me up in the Jewish tradition - my uncle Maurice was the minister in the town - to her older sister, Becky, and my father meekly went along with it.

I was upset to hear the repeated family narrative about health, the surface simple explanation, the drama that affected both of us in having an unhappy mother who was un-insightful and ignorant of basic child needs, largely because her own were probably not met too. I feel I am being as harsh in these judgements as my mother was in her judgements of me and I need to remind myself that in 1920s Oudtshoorn, Jewish immigrant families were struggling to make ends meet and apart from strict conformist adherence to Jewish traditions, had very little going for them, least of all basic and further education. Those that wanted something better for their children had to make do with long separations from their children who went to city boarding schools and universities to learn professions.

This may be the first time that I am questioning the myths and stories my mother fed us to support her self-interest and self-image. I think that my curiosity about wrong-headedness as a source of motivation, explaining bad deeds as noble gestures, and a belief in one's own essential goodness, is an illusion, which is reinforced by social certainties, a lie that gives added meaning to living, but leaves a trail of devastation and crippled lives in its wake. This must have been a powerful drive for my journey into psychoanalysis which helped repair my broken life, through increased understanding. Every time I sit with my patients, listening to their stories and their struggle to find connection to me and something positive about themselves, I feel identified with them and in some small measure, I am treating myself and my deficiencies in loving through them. Their courage in confronting pain mirrors my own efforts to heal, and in bearing witness to their transformation, I rediscover parts of myself once thought lost. The therapeutic relationship becomes a shared space of vulnerability and growth, for both of us.

Your loving Dad

Letter #5

Letter to my sister, Goldie

6ᵗʰ November 2023

Dear Goldie

I would encourage you to persevere in trying to reach James K. He is really an exceptional person, and I am sure you would enjoy and learn a lot from speaking to him. Try again.

By the way, I like your email and your take on Mum and Dad. Clearly you remember and have a much friendlier and forgiving take on them than my recollections and judgements. I agree with your accounts of them and their lives, although I think I am a little angrier than you because of the myth that was widely perpetuated that my asthma and its terrible sequelae for me were caused by Port Elizabeth's weather. I learned in my psychoanalysis, after many painful sessions, that mommy more likely simply did not like children, imposed numerous unreasonable rules, restrictions and controls on them, and when she failed, in her guilt, got others to look after them. I believe it was the controlling atmosphere in the house, the arguments and the fights over ridiculously insignificant issues, the long 3-to-5 day resentful silences, the possibility that it was the wrong marriage for her, that were the real causes of my breathlessness and my childhood asthma. I was living in terror of everything that was containing me, collapsing. Springs may have helped my asthma because it had a drier climate where I could breathe again, but Springs only produced another whole set of problems that were never dealt with.

Of course, things changed when mommy was an old woman, and she had lost her need to control. My relationship with mommy then was a whole lot easier and freer. I miss the older mother, but the younger mother was fierce, cruel, and unforgiving, and I think you and I both bore the brunt of her unhappiness. That is why I think you were so relieved every time you returned to boarding school in Cradock, and why I believe that although Springs was a disaster for me, being away from mommy was also my salvation. But that was only a partial solution, because by being sent to Springs, I also lost my truly beloved father, and perhaps you are aware of how boys are affected by losing their fathers, and, worse, being made to feel responsible for that loss. Daddy may have been angry with his property syndicate, as you say, but I do not think that caused his heart attack; I believe it was because he was made to give up everything that he had created and cherished. His anger was a silent and repressed one, occasionally erupting in a temper with mommy who goaded him with her unmet needs and frustrations. Silent anger, not expressed anger, are causes of high blood pressure and heart attacks, among other causes, of course.

I have had to accept that I was brought up in a dysfunctional family, and no amount of moralising religiosity could mask the terrible relationships and absence of love that characterised our house. Years of psychoanalysis freed me from the darkness of this craziness and as I approach the twilight years of my life, I am contented with my choices and with those around me who are close to me and who I love deeply. I am much happier in my relationships than I would otherwise have been because I love them with a boundless love as they are, warts and all, and not how I would like them to be.

Your loving brother, Mannie

Section 2

Adulthood, Restoration of my Family, and Moving from South Africa to Great Britain

Letter #6

Johannesburg (1953)

18th November 2021

Dear Shanan, Yoram & Danny

My family moved to Johannesburg in 1953 where I experienced the liberation of being in a big city. I also discovered girls and the flowering of my sexual development, which was not without its own trials and tribulations, but I managed to engage and enjoy the company of girls and even had serious 'going steady' relationships. The main thrust of my development in Johannesburg went along three pathways – my scholastic difficulties at school, my prowess in athletics and my membership of Bnei Akiva, which became my all-encompassing passion, and which I suspect, was a defence against my failures in the academic realm. I could claim proficiency over some future, unexplored phantasy goal to make up for my mediocre performance in maths and science. I ask myself how this split in my thinking and feeling, and hence my character, occurred? I later learned in my psychoanalysis that some of it originates in my phylogenetic makeup that addresses the evolutionary history and relationships within groups like heritable traits, such as DNA sequences, like the impact of the experience of being a baby in relation to a carer who carries and hands on the cultural values and ideas of tribe or clan to which they belong; and some of it belongs to my own psychological make-up – the drive for mastery, to be in control, to be noticed and liked. In other words, building my identity – this is, who I am; these are my qualities; this is how I would like to be regarded. But there is another side to these drives too, outside my consciousness – the drive to protect myself from shame and failure, from the prospect of being disliked which I half suspected was the case with people close to me on whom I depended.

I felt that my evolving religious outlook, formed in Bnei Akiva with its scouting, camping atmosphere in modern, sunny South Africa, was enlightening and airy, was outward-looking and socially and environmentally friendly. I was inspired by a new generation of rabbis who challenged the status quo in South Africa and who preached in terms of social justice and fairness for all peoples. I felt a greater kinship with them than with the white political activists who engaged in revolution and violence, but perhaps that identification with the rabbis was also a way of managing my fears of moving against the establishment to which my family strongly adhered. However, when I came to England in 1967, I was confronted by another style of Judaism – a cold, grey Germanic form of formulaic strictures, limitations and constraints and the over-bearing residues of the Holocaust that the surviving families could not escape. These communities huddled together in frightened groups, keeping their heads down, not drawing attention to themselves, not participating in the concerns of the majority. Their religiosity I saw was parochial, unsophisticated, rule-bound and with a strong fear of ostracism ('they won't eat in my house'). There were exceptions of course. Rabbi Jonathan Sacks rose above petty-minded ascetic and puritanical orthodoxies and hovered like a giant over topics of critical concern to 20th and 21st Century humanity. I admired and fought with him.

My biggest regret was to throw my lot in with the German emigrants to whose educational system you were subjected, since at the time we knew of no other or were too frightened to find out. The effect of that educational system, I believe, was to stunt your emotional development and increase your fears of outsiders. You withdrew, like I did, into a self-contained isolated intellectual ghetto, devoid of fresh thinking and courageous out-reach. To be sure, the three of you grew up to be fine loving husbands and fathers, pursuing distinguished careers of your choice in the helping professions and today you are all independent and bringing up your children in your own ways. What more could a parent ask of their children?

With love and gratitude, Dad

Letter #7

Religion - Wrong-headed thinking leading to bad things happening

7th November 2021

Dear Shanan, Yoram & Danny

I have referred in a previous Letter to the origins of my religious life at home during the 1940s which was a combination of superstitious rule-bound ideas emanating from a small-town culture in the Cape Province of South Africa, and the depressed state of my family as they heard the news coming out of Europe about the murder of 6 million Jews that included members of my father's immediate family, plus the hope and excitement that we were living in a pre-messianic era through the creation of the State of Israel, the Homeland of the Jews. As a 6- and 7-year-old, I watched everyone busily involved in the Zionist effort through supporting the fledgling State emotionally, financially and with food parcels, meetings and speeches and sending my older cousins for military training (some had served in the South African Army during WWII) prior to their travelling to join the Israeli Army. The South African Zionist movements were well-organised, and I joined the junior section of one such youth movement, Bnei Akiva. I wore my uniform proudly and learned hard for my tests to win more scouting badges. I was a good learner and follower, and I remember having the honour of standing proudly in the guard line for Rabbi Braude, Chief Rabbi of the British Empire on his visit to Springs in 1951. But those times were not all happy memories. Judaism in 1950s Eastern Transvaal was represented by bleak Lithuanian or English immigrant teachers and ministers, who were depressed and miserable, who spoke broken English and whose understanding of religion was vested in nothing more than ritualised practice and mindless recitation of blessings and prayers. Nor were they able to teach. Regular beatings with leather straps, being kept in after class and writing out lines were the usual means of controlling the class of restless, rebellious kids who went through the motions of Hebrew classes half-heartedly, mainly to manage getting through their Bar Mitzvahs. For me, I had a powerful sense of pride at achieving 'maturity' (at 13!) and taking my place in the community. I basked in the sense of specialness it gave me without thinking whether it was merited or not – the performance of ritual and to be seen performing the rituals, was everything. Wrong-headedness, the arrogance of possessing an esoteric practice that others would not or could not understand, bestowed on me a premature gravitas that made me feel elevated from other human beings. Was that what was meant by 'being closer to God'? Merely claiming, without reason, to be different and therefore superior to others? I learned this years later.

Your Loving Dad, Mannie

Letter #8

Passover

8th March 2022

Dear Adeena

It is quiet and the weather is lovely, calm and warm, inspiring pleasant thoughts about the coming day and the activities I would like to be getting on with. The 'joys of spring' is an expression that comes to mind; or having a spring in one step, or just springing forward, looking ahead, not with worry, but in anticipation. It is the festival of Passover in which one is reminded of the past most powerfully, imprinted on our collective consciousness and on personal memories of previous Passovers, with parents, recollections of family gatherings, some pleasant, others not.

There was this time, at the age 14 or 15, when my mother nagged and fussed over whether my father was reading the Haggadah, the story of the going out of Egypt, correctly. She wanted him to slow down, so that she could say every word of the Haggadah; or perhaps she thought he was skipping (passing over?) portions of the texts, and she was trying to stop him as she was trailing behind in her reading. And my father? What was he up to? What was troubling him? What was he connecting with on this Passover in which we are commanded to "remember"? Was he thinking about his family in Lithuania and the Seders that he attended as a boy in his large family, and whom he might have been remembering, who were murdered just a few short years before; or how close he was to dying, having only three years previously suffered a thrombosis. What monumental tragedies was he contemplating at this time of remembering, that were being interrupted by my mother's obsessive recitation of the Haggadah, and her grunting for him to slow down. That day had been a hard one for them both, what with shopping, Passover cleaning, cooking, instructions to the maid, preparations for the Seder table. Pressure was building up. I remember Goldie was there too, a woman of around 20. Perhaps she and I were having one of our perennial arguments over her attempts to control me and my stubborn refusal to listen to her or let her get her way.

Tension at the table was simmering. As my mother insisted again that my father should slow down, follow the right order of the recitation and rules of the Haggadah, so he would speed up - something was about to blow, and then it did. My father lashed out, knocking over the jug of salt water - meant to remind us of the tears of the Hebrew slaves in Egypt - and splashing the water over my mother, getting up and storming out the dining room, thus ending the Seder soon after it had started. My mother left to dry herself and Goldie muttered to me something about my "horrible" father and wondering why our mother ever married him. I can only guess that my subsequent attachment to religious observance and my later fixation on repairing "broken" people, the depressed and dispossessed of the world, that included the despised and murdered Jews - was a hopeless attempt to repair my parents' broken relationship, to restore and rebuild it into some imagined and phantasised ideal. The story of the Haggadah is suffused with hope of restoration and redemption, and I think I must have been driven and imbued with a desire to repair my parents' unhappy and conflict-ridden bonds that kept them tethered to each other, as Goldie and I sat there in distressed awe of their fights.

Your loving grandfather, Mannie (*)

(*) My grandchildren always called me Mannie. One day, when you were about 4, Leonie asked you to call 'oupa' for dinner. You came to the bottom of the stairs, and called up: 'Mannie, dinner's ready' and ever since I have been 'Mannie' for the grandchildren.

There is another apocryphal story of once when Nadav was about 5, he came to Leonie and said: 'Grandma, I know your name is Leonie, but what is Mannie's real name?'

Letter #9

Parenting (1960s and 1970s)

30th November 2021

Dear Shanan, Yoram & Danny

Reflecting on my role as a parent, I recall wanting to relate to my children differently to the way my parents related to me. I hoped and struggled with the twin desires of providing you with the freedoms I did not have myself, but I soon realised how limited I was in my ability to tolerate some of your childhood behaviours, demands and fears, in particular the jealousies and rivalries between you. Your early years in the late 1960s were complicated by our emigrating from South Africa to England to enable me to progress my career with further study at the London School of Economics. Emigration had weakened ties with our families. Our support came from our affiliation with the Jewish community and the beginning of my psychoanalysis. Upheavals there were aplenty, but in the face of those, we tried to maintain a reliable and stable existence for the family. Mum and I were alone, bewildered and frightened and to be sure, the rituals of life and the religion provided comfort and a sense of belonging. We survived despite moments of painful breakdown, which mum and I managed to heal and overcome through our loving partnership. You, Shanan and Yoram, experienced huge suffering during those years as you grew up and found yourselves, helped perhaps by your own psychoanalysis at the Tavistock Clinic, a process which you both found difficult, and only came to appreciate and use much later in your lives. I tried too hard to be a good father and felt deep remorse and guilt when I failed to live up to that standard and saw myself repeating patterns of behaviour that I associated with my parents. Those were the times that I began to question the role of religion in our lives and realised that I was placing religious demands above the emotional well-being of my children. I felt unable to challenge the propogandist nature of the teachings, including the myth of a God. I understood the reason for a belief in God even if I did not believe in it any longer. I felt that God is a useful focal point for turning the minds of people in a uniform direction, providing the cement that binds people together in communities and societies. The ceremonies that mark life's transitions of birth, confirmation, marriage and death I saw as providing useful symbols in the lives of people everywhere, not just in Judaism, although Jews over millennia have refined these symbols into great spiritual and inspirational wonders. The practices, rituals and ceremonies are designed to enable people to not feel alone. But I concluded people are alone in the universe, punctuated by moments of live-giving togetherness in relationships through which growth is possible. Sometimes that togetherness can turn into an unhelpful fusion of personalities that results in the loss of individuality and a suffocation of the personhood of the individual. This reminds me of the point made by the British psychoanalyst, Donald Winnicott, of the 'false self' that stems from the life-long drive of the individual to satisfy the frustrated wishes of the parent at the cost of their own development. I saw dozens of patients who would fit this category of the false self, the desire to please rather than face the terror of independence and lead lives of their own. I was like that and for years of my psychoanalysis I lived with the narcissistic belief that one day my psychoanalyst would come to see things my way, instead of me learning to see things her way.

Yours gratefully and lovingly, Dad

Letter #10

Leonie, Our Children and Our Arrival in London (August 1967)

23rd February 2022

Dear Shanan, Yoram & Danny

You, our children, Shanan, Yoram and Danny, have been the mainstay of my life that sustains me and inspires my confidence in the future through your relationships with mum and me, your commitment to our traditions, and your participation in social and communal life, in ways that bring credit to you, to Leonie and me and to our people. While I hope to be able to describe your individual personalities and styles, you have in common a wonderful, enduring sense of humour which you seem able to apply in all situations. You bring us credit and joy; you have produced families of your own and we have enjoyed wonderful times with our grandchildren.

We had you, Shanan, when mum and I were 22 and 24 respectively, and you filled our lives with joy and fun for 2 years before Yoram was born. Naturally, Yoram's arrival re-ordered the dynamics in our family relationships; we were not sophisticated, nor mature enough to be able to contend with the rivalry that ensued. I think Leonie and I each struggled to resolve our own childhood feelings and emotions through the interplay with you. The new baby, Yoram, was wondrous and a new focus of attention which we saw later was difficult for Shanan. A particular difficulty was the fact that you, Shanan, had not yet developed a vocabulary to express the upsurge of a storm of feelings around the loss of your unique place in our affections and attention. You would frequently take it out on the new baby who had displaced you as the new centre of gravity in the family. That required us to protect Yoram while at the same time recognising as far possible, the effect of this shift in dynamics for you, Shanan. We tried our best, but we must recognise that we did not always go about this very well. At the same time as this was happening, we were pursuing our studies and careers, which were in their infancy – Leonie and I were both trying to find our direction, establish ourselves in our social milieu, and fear of failing lay heavily over us. I was a student, and Leonie was a nursery schoolteacher, and she felt under pressure, from herself and from me, to seek employment and contribute to the family finances. This placed huge pressure on her, she felt torn between her love and loyalty towards her children and her commitment to her teaching role that involved providing practical and emotional support all day long to other small children in a nursery school. Soon enough we saw the effect this was having on Leonie, and the effect that her long absences from the home was having on Shanan. We realised that going back to work was premature, as both Leonie and Shanan became depressed. We decided she should cease working, which made the head of the school annoyed with us, but our increasing knowledge about the effect of early separations of mother and child helped us make the decision even at the risk of offending others – our children's needs came first.

About this time, I was coming to the end of my degree in social work, and I was making enquiries about continuing my studies at the London School of Economics in London. We now faced the possibility of another huge disruption to our family ties, support and relationships. We grew hugely anxious about how we would cope as an unsupported couple with two children in a strange country. We were taking a leap into the unknown. Looking back, we sometimes reminisce over our risky decisions, the strength of will that was required to keep things together as we strove to fulfil our ambitions. Another factor in our considerations was that we were long-standing members of the Bnei Akiva movement (https://en.wikipedia.org/wiki/Bnei_Akiva) from which we had gleaned strong ideological visions of fulfilling the Zionist dream of settling in Israel. We were also naturally committed to the type of religious life we had been educated into in the Bnei Akiva movement.

This factor influenced our decisions like where we would live in London so that we could observe the requirements of our religion and ensure that our children could attend good Jewish schools. Throughout this period (1964 - 1967) we were driven by our ambitions which were sometimes fulfilled and at other times disappointed. We were constantly in a state of conflict in attempting to satisfy the competing demands of our beliefs and principles, and our professional ambitions. Overall, we think we managed these conflicts quite well as we settled into the narrow confines of the community of German emigrants in Northwest London, while studying and working in the secular world in which I was becoming more interested and entrenched. Leonie completed her nursery schoolteacher training and was employed in the nursery school of the German-Jewish community which was noted for their concentration on the minutiae of religious practice. We fitted in reasonably well and made new friends with parents of the children in the nursery school, who were by and large second-generation immigrants and who practiced a more reasonable and progressive form of Judaism, more in line with our Bnei Akiva standards.

I completed the Diploma in Psychiatric Social Work at the London School of Economics in 1968. At the time, the Seebohm Commission was planning the liquidation of social work specialisms and recommending their integration into one all-embracing Local Authority and Allied Personal Social Services. The unitary department included services provided by children's departments, welfare services, home help services, mental health, social work services and social care functions provided by other organisations. I was critical of the new structures insofar as they weakened the one social work method that I was interested in, viz. casework, that was oriented towards understanding the inner emotional and psychological development of people in addition to 'fixing' broken individuals and families. Seebohm became one of the reasons why I decided to train as a psychoanalytical psychotherapist, and I was fortunate in 1971 to be offered a post in the Adult Department of the Tavistock Clinic which provided me with the right training to integrate my social work persona with my desire to delve into and work with the mysteries of the individual and collective mind.

Adjusting to a 'British way of thinking' in 1967 was not without its difficulties. I felt that moving to Britain would provide me with opportunities that had been denied to me in South Africa. I recall at university in Johannesburg in 1961 learning about the Elizabethan Poor Laws of 1601, that were administered through parish overseers, to provide relief for the aged, sick, and infant poor, as well as work for the able-bodied in workhouses. It seemed to me that this legislation reflected a level of civilised society because of the care shown to its weaker members through collective social action. This, I felt, was most admirable; it was very different from the South African milieu where provision for the poor was left to local charities catering primarily for their own cultural and religious groups.

After graduating from the London School of Economics in 1968, I was worked as a psychiatric social worker at the new Barnet Child Guidance Centre, and it was during this time that my interest in training as a psychoanalyst was stimulated. Talking to as many people as I could, attending the Porchester Winter Lectures organised by the Institute of Psychoanalysis, led me to apply for the training in psychoanalysis, but my first application (and later my second application) was turned down – I was hugely disappointed. I had never felt so awful in my life because in some ways I was 'spoiled', expecting to receive whatever I had set my mind on. I thought then that my next step was to start my psychoanalytic treatment – that would get me in – but I was to discover that was part of my wrong-headed thinking – that if I did 'A', I would automatically get 'B'. I learned that psychoanalysis was not something one acquired like a credit; it was a journey that first demanded my recognition and acceptance that there was something really the matter with me that needed attention. There were no shortcuts; I really had to face the deep flaws in my personality and thinking and commit to learning about them (and change them) without having the ulterior motive of acquiring a cloak of professionalism and the status that would come from being a psychoanalyst. I had to look in the mirror as honestly as I could and engage truthfully and in a disciplined way, with a psychoanalyst and open my mind and feelings to her and about her in the context of the psychoanalytic relationship. Putting it another way, I had to face and deal with my own deficiencies and shortcomings before I could hope to deal with the deficiencies of others. So, in 1969, I settled into my own 5-times-a-week Kleinian-oriented psychoanalytic treatment in which I remained for 9 years, during which time we had our third son, Danny, in 1972. Around that time, Leonie too started her own Kleinian psychoanalysis. Our lives were filled mainly with daily journeys to our sessions, taking and collecting the children from their nursey schools and providing for them. We had incomes from our jobs, but we needed additional financial support from our parents. We were living on the breadline for years, never took holidays because most of our funds supported our psychoanalyses. We were hugely grateful to our psychoanalysts for charging us low fees. The psychoanalytic experience was painful and raised stubborn resistances in me that lasted, I remember, about 3 years. I had not realised how deeply embedded were my arrogant and omnipotent defences that I had built up over a lifetime of thinking I was special and entitled and now I had to learn a new language, a new way of thinking about myself and everything about me including what my Judaism truly meant for me and how I related to it and used it. Even practical decision-making and problem-solving came under the psychoanalytic microscope. I was horrified to discover the extent of the unresolved emotional limitations of my childhood, how my flights of fancy fed my narcissism, how I displaced my inner conflicts onto Leonie and my children. My drives towards a spurious autonomy, managing my fears and my own unrecognised rivalry with others, including my children, drove me to my wits end – I did not know how to deal with these feelings, but my psychoanalyst stuck with me, she did not reject me which was my biggest fear – that my early childhood separation from my mother (and father) would be repeated with my psychoanalyst and between me and my children. Opening myself to these fears in the real context of the here-and-now of the psychoanalysis, as distinct from learning about them from reading books, made me face my denied weaknesses, but this also led me into constant battles with my psychoanalyst. At times, I felt that she despaired of me, perhaps like my mother must have despaired of me as I struggled to get out from under her domination. By about the third year of my psychoanalysis, I think I accepted that the fight with my psychoanalyst was pointless and self-defeating and limited the possibilities of my growth and development. I learnt to co-operate with her, to consider what she was saying to me, which were more accurate reflections of my emotional state of mind than I could have come up with, and which provided me with new understandings of myself.

Yours thoughtfully, Mannie

Letter #11

Mixed feelings about Separation and Christian National Education

16th December 2021

Dear Shanan, Yoram & Danny

Reflecting on what I wrote to you earlier, one imagines a deeply unhappy, repressed, unimaginative child. This was not the case. I recall participating in the discussions, plans and the moves back and forth between my family and my uncle and aunt in 1947-52. There was excitement and adventure too, explorations and naughtiness. The good feelings at the renewal of the relationships with my mother on my return to Port Elizabeth lasted about 2-3 days – before critical negative feelings crept into our relationship again over her anxious controlling behaviour towards me. But I ask myself, I have drive and motivation, and I know how to apply myself to prolonged and hard work – that must have come from somewhere. Although scholastically I was mediocre, I discovered I was successful in athletics in the middle-distance races, and I focussed more on that than on my schoolwork. My academic blossoming started when I got to university in Johannesburg in 1961. But before that, I was a product of South Africa's Nationalist Government's Christian National Education.

Christian National Education – (1940s to 1950s)

I still feel today that I am hobbled by the South African Calvinistic Christian National Educational school system – an example of 'wrong-headed' thinking leading to bad things happening.

The religious education curriculum in South African schools was based on Calvinistic teaching of the Afrikaans Dutch Reformed Church in relation to the Bible, God, Sin and Salvation. Religious education subject matter was strictly Christian and aimed at converting young people to the Christian faith. Teachers would be expected to be committed Christians and a member of the Church. This caused serious problems - the evangelical and Calvinistic ethos of Christian National Education caused young people and teachers to adopt a negative attitude towards it, and in my case, to turn defiantly and arrogantly to my own religion, Judaism, which to my mind, was a superior form of faith and outlook.

The concept of education in South Africa required the teacher to acknowledge God as the Sovereign Creator in whose image all human beings are made - teachers were expected to see God's hand in all they do and say, whether it is in teaching religious education, history or physics. The educator is expected to recognise the authority of God and learn from his revelation as found in the Bible. Notions such as objectivity and neutrality were irrelevant; They were seen as falsehoods which hide the truth of the Gospel from young people. National Christian Education was based on the concept of converting pupils to Christianity, for committed Christian service to the country, whether as doctors, lawyers, teachers, etc., and for active participation in their Church. There was little room for critical thought and debate; thinking was reduced to the limiting dogmas of faith, and to challenge that was risky.

In the dynamics of large human systems like cities and states, the social and cultural attitudes of the majority tend to seep into the minds and educational systems of the minority – the non-Christian faiths. I am certain that my mother's education, although it occurred before the introduction of formal Christian National Education in 1948, and mine, when it did, were influenced by the stringent, harsh purist attitudes of the prevailing dominant Christian culture of the time. Jewish education too was suffused with similar ideas of God's hand in creation and in daily life, as espoused in the Bible. Superiority and separateness in Judaism, which although it developed in its own way, mirrored the superiority and separateness of Afrikaner Christendom. The State schools in South Africa, of which mine were a part, were conducted according to colour and race. There were no racially mixed schools. Separate schools, like the Jewish schools, contended that there would be chaos because of a conflict of cultures - an excuse used to keep the different races and religions separate, based on the ideology of avoiding 'mongrelising' the races and assuming for each race group, the cultural environment of the child.

Beneath all, lay the belief of the Afrikaner in racial superiority (for this, in my family, read Jewish superiority). For three centuries this belief dominated the religious wrong-headed thinking of the religious educational curricula in South African schools. Each race group was meant to develop according to its own cultural or racial way. Modern educational concepts and theories of teaching religious education aimed at aiding children to contact other cultures, was not supported by the State. Such theories were regarded with suspicion because they might have led to the rejection of the State ideology of "separate development" by pupils. The Christian curriculum was based on the idea of helping children accept their identity. There was to be no room for children to agonize over secular questions. Issues of the pass laws, Homeland's, the Immorality Act, that prohibited sexual relations between white people and people of other races, etc., were not to be discussed in religious education classes, or in other subject lessons, and they were not discussed at home. So, although my parents views corresponded with the prevailing views on race relations of the official Afrikaner Nationalist Government, in the general elections they supported the opposition United Party. In fact, my father was a local activist, visiting homes in the area seeking people's votes for the United Party. It seemed to me that the United Party, comprising mainly English speakers, was only slightly less extreme in its race policies than the Nationalist Party which was comprised mainly of Afrikaans speakers. When I told my parents that I was intending to vote for the Progressive Party, a party to the left of the United Party, that promised voting and other human rights to the non-white races, they were disappointed in my choice, but they did not prevent me from exercising my rights to vote as I wished.

Sincerely, Dad

Section 3
My Professional Journey - Social Work, Psychiatric Social Work, Psychotherapy & Organisational Consultancy

Letter #12

Mary Barker (1971 to 1987)

10th October 2021

Dear Shanan, Yoram & Danny

One of my supervisors at the Tavistock Clinic during the 1970s, and who became my consultant during the 1980s, after I had left the Clinic, was Mary Barker. She had a tranquil, magisterial personality, nothing flustered her, yet she was firm and resolved about what needed doing and how to get there. She had a keen sense of humour but was also serious and did not suffer fools or obstreperous boys like me, gladly. She was blessed with foresight that enabled her to view social trends prophetically five years in advance and alert others to prepare for them. Mary must have seen a budding writing talent in me. "One publication a year" she said, and that is what I have done since then. Writing is risky because one is communicating with an unseen audience and there is no way of anticipating its reactions. Mary helped me face and overcome both my omnipotence and chronic doubt that I experienced in everything I wrote. She helped me with my first publication and got me my first part-time lectureship at Brunel University in 1977. Mary became a good friend and an excellent role model. From her I learnt how to adapt the working psychiatric social work/psychotherapy models I had internalised while still holding true to core theoretical roots. When Mary was hospitalised with a serious illness, she arranged for her Kleinian psychoanalyst to visit her at the hospital at 06.00 three mornings a week, where in a quiet room just off the ward, taken there by a nurse, she would present her dreams for analysis. This, she told me, provided her with strength through the day of pain and difficult treatments. This arrangement between them lasted until she died. I learned from Mary that context may change, but values, empathy and compassion are the central elements in the psychotherapeutic relationship, as in all relationships.

Browsing the Internet, I discovered this obituary to Mary Barker by Margaret Richards published in *Social Work Education*, 7:2, 28-28, 1988. I am including it here because it describes the Mary I knew so well.

Obituary

Mary Barker - A Personal Appreciation

I was one of Mary Barker's many learners, initially as a newly appointed manager, in the early days of Seebohm when she convened a group to examine leadership issues; and more recently as a participant in the workshop for social work educators, of which she was a co-leader. In both experiences the most profound learning came from being able to observe, challenge, discuss issues of leadership with someone who could not only present her own unique formulations, but could demonstrate them in the here-and-now of the learning group.

In the first place was her calm and lucidity, her capacity to offer her material and views with minimum jargon or fuss; secondly, was her recognition of the need to bring negative feelings out into the open, and the positive non-paranoid way that she could handle conflict and aggression.

But it was the creativity that she generated which most impressed me and for which I am most indebted. She had already written about the use of drawing, and its potential in a variety of work settings to make accessible different layers of meaning. But it was her enthusiasm for her own newly discovered talent for painting that was instrumental in getting me, a total non-artist, to begin to enjoy painting for its own sake. Her pleasure was infectious. I can remember a seascape she showed us, the colours suggested by a pebble brought home from holiday, and the way I was inspired with the zest to experiment for myself.

When she was already seriously ill, a group of us from the Education Workshop met at her flat to pool resources to edit and publish course members' papers as a book which emerged as *Educating Social Workers*. Her calm and unhurried contribution conveyed such a sense of confidence in the project, upon which her pain and illness were not allowed to intrude.

I am sad that she is gone. It is hard that someone who had so much to give should die so young. At a personal and professional level, she will be very much missed.

Mary Richards

NISW

My relationship with Mary intensified and expanded my understanding of the professional helping relationship. It helped me give up the all-consuming compulsion to solve everyone's problems and I developed greater respect for the concept of boundaries and their implied limitations and their role in mental health. The helping relationship merits greater study – it is not a sentimental helping of others out of their woes and misfortune, but it is the application of careful assessment and taking account of other influences in clients'/patients' lives and character that can be mobilised to create a supportive structure and environment for the development of independence. I have often wondered about the origin of my urge to help others, but I also recognise that the urge to help in people contributes to the social cohesion of communities. Once, in a consultation session with Mary, I was talking about the recent death of my father, when I was overwhelmed with deep sadness for what my father represented, which was over and above my personal loss. We talked about the period of history in which my father had lived in Lithuania that had forced him to move, alone, to a strange land at the age of twenty-seven, learn a new language, train in cabinetmaking, and make enough of a living to marry, have a family and start a business. He was a kind man, quiet but determined, but also a product of his time, firstly, in Eastern Europe at the turn of the Century, and later in a provincial city in South Africa, carrying in him a semi-permanent sense of sadness, probably because he suspected, and which was later confirmed, that his siblings who had not managed to emigrate from Lithuania, had been murdered during the War. Seven decades later I travelled to Uzventis, my father's hometown in Lithuania, to discover the details of their demise and to stand by a raised mound in the forest, their mass grave, and recite the Kaddish, the Jewish prayer of mourning and remembrance.

My perspective on religion underwent a significant transformation through my conversations with Mary and as a result of my experiences in psychoanalysis and group relations conference work. Initially, I held rigid views shaped by guilt and a sense of responsibility for historical and cultural narratives. I saw religious concepts, like the Messiah, as absolute truths that I wasn't meant to question. However, as I explored these beliefs more deeply, I began to see them differently.

I started to understand that my messianic beliefs were, in part, a psychological defence mechanism—a way to cope with the inherent helplessness and dependency of human existence, especially as seen through the lens of early childhood experiences. This realization led me to view messianic ideas as delusional when taken to extreme, psychotic levels of mental and group functioning.

This shift allowed me to relax my rigid stance on religion and explore new perspectives. I no longer felt compelled to adhere strictly to dogma or feel responsible for the "tides of history." Instead, I became more open to questioning and reinterpreting religious beliefs, understanding them as complex cultural constructs rather than unassailable truths. This change in perspective brought a sense of relief and freedom, enabling me to adopt a more flexible and nuanced view of religion and its role in my life.

Your loving father, Mannie

Letter #13

Dorothea Brande on *Becoming a Writer*

15th January 2022

Dear Shanan, Yoram & Danny

It took me two or three sittings to read Dorothea Brande's book: *Becoming a Writer*. The book was written in 1934 and yet it was as fresh and relevant as if it had just been published. Her approach resembles that of our Masterclass tutor, Jacqueline Burns, by encouraging different parts of the brain/mind/thoughts/emotions to find expression through the exercise of writing whatever comes into one's mind without effort, control, or censorship. In this way, writing resembles the psychoanalytic technique of free association, speaking to one's psychoanalyst about whatever passes through one's mind without shame or embarrassment. The purpose of doing this is to enable access to the unconscious parts of the mind, to free the creative sides of oneself by acknowledging repressed thoughts, fears and desires and make them part of one's conscious life and available for use in everyday life. I am absolutely in favour of Dorothea Brande's depiction of the writer as having two personalities, then three personalities in one that must be brought into harmony through the discipline and routine of regular writing periods, usually, but not only, best in the first hours of the morning before the day's events and outside influences intrude and command the attention of the conscious, decision-oriented, judging aspects of oneself. Free-floating thoughts from that part of the self that is the antithesis of the usually busy, alert and commanding part of the self is a wonderful talent to develop if one hopes to be a serious writer.

Like others this morning, I slept poorly last night, unable to fall asleep and then waking at 3.00am. Perhaps it has something to do with the meetings of the writing Masterclass that generates anxiety the night before because of all the many disconnected thoughts swirling in my mind which I am trying to bring out onto paper. I had a dream during the night, which I can barely remember but which involved the presence of some men in grey suits in a school classroom and me trying unsuccessfully to 'fit in' to their group. I think one man said, 'come in; we will make room for you', but that did not happen. My associations to the dream involve a series of WhatsApps during the day between my three sons, each reminiscing hilariously about their experiences at primary school and their abominable teachers who were often violent and sadistic, throwing hard objects at children, wrestling them to the floor, as a form of maintaining control. Leonie and I felt permanently guilty for having sent them to that school, but we were new in the country, and we opted for the first school we came across.

Yours, etc, Mannie

Letter #14

Writing

16th June 2022

Dear Adeena

Write, write, write! Get your ideas out onto the page in any form you like - whole sentences or jumbled words - find a way to let your thoughts rise, formulate and travel to your fingertips for transmission onto the blank paper. I have discovered a liking for pages without lines so I can roam anywhere on the page I like without restriction. This reminds me of my early years at school, learning to write with pencil, then with nibbed pen, dipped in Stephen's ink, and the tall stern teacher, Miss Frankin, walking about the classroom with a ruler in one hand ready to smack children across the palm of their hands if their writing violated spaces by crossing over the lines, except the letters 'f', 'g', 'j', 'p' 'q', 'y' and 'z'. This type of education was meant to produce disciplined and conforming children, and so it did, at the expense of expansiveness, discovery, courage, risk-taking and personal responsibility. These creative qualities have been newly discovered in me at this late stage of my life because of the help of so many people who have influenced my development. In the autumn of my life, I have discovered with gratitude the joys of freedom that comes from the lifting of the shadows of guilt. I feel I am a responsible husband and father and grandfather, citizen and professional, while at the same time, I am aware of a destructive negative and unhelpful side to me that needs controlling (Keep between the lines! I hear Miss Frankin). I am forever grateful to Grandma, my two psychoanalysts, many supervisors, consultants, colleagues and collaborators, who provided the necessary emotional containment (the 'human lines') that enabled me to explore all aspects of my personality, history and contexts, including thoughts, impulses, faith and politics. These human interactive relationships have permitted me to accept the characteristics and limitations of my own genuine and authentic self, and free myself as far as possible from imposed regulation, and the desire to seek approval from others. The social context in which this transformation has taken place is important too - it was not in Israel which I had idealised and dreamed of throughout my adolescence, although Israel still figures importantly in my heart, but it is Great Britain, which despite its many internal difficulties and negative aspects of its history in different parts of the world, is committed to creating a just and fair society through its admirable political systems and social institutions.

In 2010, as the last Labour Government of Gordon Brown was approaching an election, I called Number 10 Downing Street to enquire whether and how the Tavistock Institute of Human Relations could better help understand the society that the Labour Party was hoping to continue governing. The speed with which my request was responded to pointed to a level of desperation in the Prime Minister's residence. I was invited to come to Number 10. Now it was me who panicked - how do I get into Number 10? So, I asked the person at the other end of the telephone, and she replied, "You ring the bell".

With rising trepidation, a colleague and I walked up to the door at Number 10 and rang the bell, told the receptionist whom we were there to see and within minutes we were ushered into a meeting room with the Health and Social Care Advisor to the Prime Minister. The Advisor was sufficiently interested in what the Tavistock Institute had to offer in the evaluation of social attitudes and their impact on the Government's social policies, that he suggested we have a second meeting at the Tavistock Institute offices. For this meeting, I asked 7 or 8 Tavistock Institute researchers and consultants to join.

Two things stand out from this meeting: (i) the Government Adviser could not stop eating the biscuits and he finished off the whole plate without offering any to the others. This behaviour suggested to us the presence of widespread anxiety bordering on panic in Number 10. (ii) When the late Dr Dione Hills asked the Advisor if the Labour Party ever "listens to the people", he replied tersely, "no, that way would lead to chaos". We were appalled to hear this reply, and, in that moment, we realised Labour was going to lose the election and there was not much point in continuing the conversation. It dawned on us (perhaps we should have known this) that when a political party reaches the highest point of its powers, a delusional state of mind can infect the whole hierarchy. It seemed natural for the Advisor to admit to a practice that he would never have acknowledged had the Party not been in power. Perhaps the reason was that they had been so battered by the electorate that they could not bear to listen to it any longer. It also seemed a classic case of "power corrupts, and absolute power corrupts absolutely" appearing before our disbelieving eyes. It was a lesson for us on how easily political parties can lose touch with the people who had put them there, and how our fragile democratic structures are so dependent on the psychology and emotions of the people and their leaders.

In the aftermath of this unsettling encounter, we were left with a deep sense of unease about the state of our political system. The Advisor's peculiar behaviour and dismissive attitude revealed a troubling detachment from the very citizens who hold the power to shape the government. It was a stark reminder that even the most well-intentioned administrations can become ensnared in the trappings of power, losing sight of their foundational principles. The experience underscored the vital importance of maintaining a vigilant and engaged citizenry, capable of holding their leaders accountable. As we walked away, we couldn't shake the feeling that we had witnessed a pivotal moment in political history—a moment where the facade of control cracked, exposing the underlying chaos and fear. It served as a cautionary tale about the perils of unchecked authority and the necessity of continual reflection and humility in leadership. In the end, this encounter was not just about the failings of one party but a broader lesson on the fragility of our democratic institutions and the critical role of public oversight in preserving their integrity.

Your loving Grandfather, Mannie

Letter #15

Writing

4th April 2023.

Dear Shanan, Yoram & Danny

I have neglected writing to you for weeks which I regret, but I am confounded by so many other crises that are happening in and around me. Writing is a tranquillizer, calming me in a turbulent sea of change, pressure and unpredictability. Luckily, Leone is by my side with a solid grasp of reality, with organising skills, that keep me grounded and focused on what needs to be done.

Firstly, there is an existential war raging in the Middle East which impacts directly on my family. Nadav, my grandson, is an officer in the engineering battlegroup in Gaza, whose task, I imagine is to find and destroy the tunnels which hide the Hamas terrorists and serve as surprise exit points from which they emerge and ambush. I imagine he operates the foam bombs that fill the tunnels and solidify quickly to cut off Hamas from their fighting objectives. We worry and pray for Nadav's safety and the family from loss. The tragic conflict in the Middle East and its repercussions in the rest of the world, the simplistic splitting into good and bad, no longer make sense if looked at in isolation. I do my best to hold onto my professional/philosophical views that look at conflict as a basic human drive and part of the necessary civilising processes we go through to live reasonably with each other in our families, communities and in the world, and on the only planet in the universe probably capable of sustaining life. It is utterly bewildering, therefore, that human beings suffer from a Samson-like complex that is capable of 'bringing the house down' and destroying everything, even ourselves, because hatred of each other is so intensely driven that even self-preservation drives are overwhelmed, and we dive willingly into oblivion, a wild rage that destroys all rational thought and logic, a collective narcissism that is at the centre of religion. Our so-called enlightenment really posits that we are hardly more advanced than a herd of rampaging savage animals.

The other source of worry is my kidney dialysis treatment, which has moved from hospital to home. This is a big step. And it is turning out to be more complex than I had thought. Admittedly, it is only but one day. And it is to be expected that there would be glitches to iron out before the process can run well. My nurse, Arnel, the technician, Lindsay, were on hand to iron out problems and help me when I needed it. Not everything that was needed was in place at the start of the treatment and we decided to press on anyway. The reclining chair is the biggest disappointment because I cannot reach the controls of the dialyzing machine from a sitting position, which is necessary in the event of my blood pressure falling rapidly. The new chair that is being made for me can only be raised by another inch or two, but 6 to 8 inches more height is required. We think building a wooden plinth will solve that problem. Other things that need attention are installing a light, a clock, an alarm bell, and a plastic covering for the carpet around the chair. One big concern is how to troubleshoot. Should the alarm on the dialyser go off, instructions appear on the control panel screen on what measures to take to remedy the problem, but the alarm raises panic, and my thinking becomes paralysed.

Your loving Dad

Letter #16

On Writing

16 December 23

Dear Goldie

I recall the phrase the "thinking hand" that is attributed to some writers. I have noticed when I start writing, at some point, my hand takes over, and it produces words and sentences that seem independent of my mind. The output just flows, sentence after sentence, and an outline narrative appears. Of course, the origin of the thought lies in my mind and gets transmitted to my hand, but equally, the sensation is that my hand is running along independently. Speech, on the other hand is different; instead, I find often there is a disconnection between my mind and speech, more hesitation, more repression, or more showing off. Care has to be taken in choosing the right words, tone and intent of the communication. This calculation is due, not simply, to the importance of being civil in my communications, or being accurate in how I describe my needs. The sense is more like a heaviness, a fear of judgement of aspects of myself like weakness or guilt.

I am thinking this because I wrote a from-the-heart e-mail to you and you did not reply, which is unlike you. I suspect you were upset by my e-mail because it was a critique of our early family life which paints our mother in negative terms as a mother who did not like children, was envious of them, and through her angry, controlling personality, destroyed the family. My e-mail probably punctured your idealised picture of our family and our ancestors.

I sometimes wonder why I have left it so late in my life to come out with this stuff. This is where I think the idea of the "thinking hand" comes in. My writing represents a form of expression that comes from a different part of my brain than speech. In many ways, it is like revealing the recesses of one's mind in psychoanalysis through speaking thoughts and dreams openly and honestly, without censorship, and listening and working with the interpretations offered by one's psychoanalyst. But even in that intense relationship, a degree of withholding thoughts occurs, either because of shame or guilt.

Two factors come together here - firstly, I started having psychotherapy for the second time to deal with the problems of ageing, decline in health and mental ability, and feelings about my approaching death. Secondly, I recently attended a course in non-fiction writing because I wish to leave something worthwhile to my children and grandchildren. The course teacher helpfully steered the students away from censorship, encouraged forthright expression and bravery in revealing to the world that which lies deep within our unconscious motivations and other drives. Naturally, one censors because exposure may produce negative pushback, or the hurt that could be caused to others, and further fracture relationships. Censoring can be done later during editing for publication.

In the complex arrangements of relations in families it often happens that certain individuals will unconsciously be 'selected' to carry specific emotional and behavioural manifestations that can be said to be done 'on behalf of' other members of the family, who can then eschew these behaviours as not belonging to them. For example, the parents who push their children to excel educationally because they had had a poor education, or the child of ill parents, who dreams of becoming a doctor or nurse, who unconsciously hopes thereby to treat and heal the sick parents through the care of patients. Or not unlike the child of anxious parents taking up a career in social work or psychotherapy, or the child who adopts delinquency as a reaction to parents who obsess about goodness and salvation as a means of denying their own suppressed desires for rebellion.

In reflecting on these intricate family dynamics and my recent explorations in writing and psychotherapy, I find that the concept of the "thinking hand" resonates with me. Writing has become an outlet for unearthing and confronting the unspoken truths of our shared past, truths that speech often fails to capture with the same honesty and clarity. The act of writing, unlike speech, allows for a freer expression of thoughts and emotions, often revealing hidden layers of understanding and insight. This process, akin to a psychoanalytic journey, has brought forth revelations about our family history that challenge long-held perceptions and idealizations. While this candid exploration risks causing discomfort and potentially straining relationships, it is also a necessary path toward authenticity and reconciliation. By confronting these painful realities and acknowledging the complex interplay of our familial roles and expectations, I hope to foster a more nuanced understanding and healing. In this endeavour, I strive to balance the need for honesty with compassion, recognizing that while the truths unearthed may be difficult to accept, they are an essential part of our collective narrative.

Your loving brother, Mannie

Section 4
My Psychoanalytic Treatment

Letter #17

The First Dream

30th August 2021

Dear Shanan, Yoram & Danny

It was 1967 - the first dream of my psychoanalysis was shocking. It revealed a part of me that I thought I had left behind and expunged for good. I believed I was now a fully liberal, tolerant person because I had rejected the race attitudes of the society I had grown up in South Africa; I had moved to a 'fair' Britain to be part of an egalitarian and democratic society, and I thought I was doing well in it. I could not believe what my psychoanalyst was telling me that the dream revealed a disregard for my black servants as taken-for-granted people whose sole purpose was to serve my needs; that my puffed-up state of mind was such that I expected to be provided for without making any effort myself and, my psychoanalyst said, moreover, I was treating her too in similar fashion as a nanny whom I expected to be available at all times, or as an audience meant to applaud my superior refined social attitudes.

The tone and content of my psychoanalysis followed these themes for 9 years – the struggle to support what was increasingly an unsustainable self-image and the attempts to persuade my psychoanalyst that I was right, and she was wrong. Only after about three years was I able to let go of the struggle, stop the fighting, and listen carefully to what she was gently offering me as alternative ways of thinking about myself, my relationships and the direction my life was taking. The changes were not easy to make, and I frequently regressed to my old self-centred self which came at huge cost to mum and you three growing children. Dependency and weakness had become synonymous in my mind with defeat and surrender, and I fought hard against these feelings, and I abhorred them in others. Yet, in my work as a psychiatric social worker and later as a psychotherapist, I felt compassion and an ardent desire to help those who needed my help. A split had occurred in me – tolerance of weakness in my clients/patients and a fierce intolerance of similar feelings in myself and in the family. I wanted you, my sons, to be everything I was not, which I believe caused you difficulties in your development and in your social relationships. I saw you seeking acceptance from your peers in middle class environments of your school and synagogue, while I was elsewhere, out in the world, and in my mind, working with people who had not had similar opportunities to experience and develop as I had, because we still inhabited a deeply class-ridden society. And yet, at the same time I had difficulty accepting that my mind was constructed along class lines too in ways that inevitably placed me in a superior position, a know-it-all who would bring knowledge and light to all. Humility, if there was any, expressed itself instead as self-doubt, because setting the bar so high for my goals, meant that I feared failure was inevitable.

To be sure, the path I had chosen was satisfyingly therapeutic. I learned to be patient, tolerant and forgiving through the support I received from others – mum, who kept reminding me that she was not my enemy, you who grew up to face your life's tribulations with fortitude and determination, my two psychoanalysts and several supervisors of my work, bosses, consultants and colleagues who shared their knowledge with consistent kindness. They and you made me feel wanted and useful and importantly, they provided a framework in which I could let go of aspects of my narcissism and outdated doctrines and open myself to new ways of thinking that released me from having to provide answers about everything to everyone. I could be kinder to myself and be more tolerant of my limitations.

I recognize that my journey through psychoanalysis and self-exploration has been a profound and often painful process of uncovering truths about myself and my relationships. The initial shock of that first dream in 1967 set the stage for a nine-year struggle to reconcile the discrepancies between my self-image and the underlying attitudes I carried from my upbringing in South Africa. My psychoanalyst's insights challenged me to confront a deeply ingrained sense of superiority and an unrealistic expectation of being served without reciprocation. The resistance I felt toward accepting these revelations was formidable, manifesting in a relentless effort to defend my constructed identity. However, as I gradually let go of this defensive stance, I learned to listen and consider alternative perspectives, allowing for significant personal growth.

This process also revealed a profound split within me: a compassionate professional side dedicated to helping others and a private self that was intolerant of vulnerability, both in myself and my family. This contradiction caused strain, particularly in my relationships with you and mum. I acknowledge that my high expectations and fear of dependency may have created challenges for you, as you navigated your own paths within a society that I critiqued yet unwittingly embodied.

Ultimately, the support and understanding from those around me, including family, psychoanalysts, and colleagues, have been instrumental in my growth. They offered a safe space to question and dismantle outdated beliefs, fostering a more forgiving and patient approach to life. Through this, I've learned to embrace my limitations and let go of the need to have all the answers. This journey has not only been therapeutic but has also enabled me to cultivate a deeper sense of humility and empathy, both toward others and myself. It is a continuous process, one that remains essential as I continue to evolve and understand the complexities of my own psyche.

Your loving Dad, Mannie

Letter #18

A Dream

11th February 2022

Dear Shanan, Yoram and Danny

I had a disturbing dream during the night. It involved betrayal, sex and violence and it unfolded like it was inevitable. I could not stop events from happening – the seduction, the retribution, the threats to my life, my hopeless attempts to sweet talk the killers out of their intention to torture me and then kill me. And it was all taking place in very pleasant surroundings, a sunny day, and in a picturesque village, walks in what looked like hot, desert-like countryside, all the while hoping that the killers would change their minds, given that they were well-dressed in suits and came from the same tribe as me. Why would they kill me? I had broken tribal customs and code of honour by being sexually involved with the leader's woman. The killer's weapons of torture were screwdrivers. I was given one too, as if tempting me to chance a breakout which would give them reason to finish me off. My associations to this dream lead me to a recent lecture by my colleague, Leslie Brissett, on the European Colonialist Project that supported supremacist dynamics viz a viz other cultures and races for 2,000 years. Leslie concentrated on the end of the Holy Roman Empire during the Dark Ages and the on-going role of the Catholic Church in controlling the affairs of state and its campaign of intimidation, theft, torture and death against those who did not accept the supreme sovereignty of the Church, through its Office of the Inquisitions. The main target of the Inquisition were the Jews, but Leslie made no mention of them or of antisemitism. Another person in the audience brought up the question of the Jews and spoke about the Torah and her reference to the Torah made me think about the Torah's opposition to slavery, the Torah stipulating care of the environment, not to mention its approach to social justice, equality before the law for everyone and so on. I castigated myself for not speaking up, but the dynamic in the lecture was such that I felt unable to speak (be potent) because of a fear of a backlash, so I lost out in my silence, and I would have lost out if I had spoken (I was screwed).

Another Dream

I dreamt I was at my synagogue, wandering around and greeting people. I passed a bookshelf with old books stacked on the shelves. Standing next to the bookshelf, oddly placed in the middle of the hall, was our old friend P. He explains to me that the books belonged to his late father, a psychiatrist, and they date from the 1930s/1940s. I peek inside one tome and I see that it is a psychiatric textbook, rather dusty, but nevertheless, pertinent to our current understanding of mental illness. I leave P and start to exit the synagogue, and I notice that I am not wearing my jacket; I had removed it and left it somewhere in the synagogue. I remember thinking as I got home that I was missing my jacket and that later, inconveniently, I would have to return to the synagogue to retrieve it. The dream reminds me of P's wife, K., and the occasional meals we had at their home. Those meals were devastatingly boring as we had to listen to endless accounts of K's experiences at work, and other everyday matters about friends, shopping, the house, her children, delivered in the loftiest, supremely ecstatic superlatives, the peaks of perfection, the acme of achievement, the 'best', 'the finest', 'the most beautiful', 'the most wonderful', etc. I would be drowning in her idealisation of everything, and yet we knew she had serious worries about her 'brilliant' children, one of whom was behaving oddly. What went on there? Who knows? Intriguing, and to cover it up, K. blathered on and on about the faultlessness of everything and everyone. Her sad face probably told the true story of what was going on inside her.

The dreams described in this letter can be seen as symbolic representations of my inner conflicts, fears, and unresolved issues. Here's a deeper interpretation of the symbolism in each dream:

Betrayal, Violence, and Retribution: The dream's theme of betrayal, involving a relationship with a tribal leader's woman, could symbolize a transgression against established norms or values. This might reflect my feelings of guilt or fear of judgment for breaking away from societal or cultural expectations, perhaps related to my past in South Africa and my rejection of supremacist attitudes.

The impending violence and torture by members of my own 'tribe' suggest a fear of punishment for my perceived wrongdoing. The use of screwdrivers as instruments of torture might symbolize a sense of being "screwed" or trapped by the consequences of my actions. The well-dressed appearance of the killers adds an element of irony, suggesting that the threat can come from within one's own community or people who appear respectable.

The juxtaposition of a sunny day and a picturesque village with the violent narrative highlights a discord between outward appearances and underlying tensions. It may symbolize my awareness of the hidden dangers or hypocrisies within seemingly peaceful or normal environments.

My attempts to sweet-talk the killers suggests a sense of powerlessness and desperation to escape the consequences of my actions or an internal struggle to reconcile with past mistakes or to seek forgiveness.

In the second dream the synagogue, a place of worship and community symbolizes my connection to a specific cultural and religious identity. The presence of old psychiatric textbooks suggests a reflection on mental health, possibly hinting at a search for understanding or a grappling with psychological issues in which I have been engaged over a lifetime.

The act of leaving behind a jacket could symbolize a sense of loss or something missing in my life. It may represent a loss of protection, identity, or security, prompting the need to return to the synagogue (my roots?) to retrieve it.

The memories of dull, idealized conversations with K. reflect a tension between outward appearances and inner reality. I perceive K.'s exaggerated praise as a cover for deeper, unspoken anxieties, perhaps mirroring my own struggle with presenting a façade instead of confronting uncomfortable truths.

K.'s face hints at hidden suffering or the toll that maintaining a perfect image can take on a person. This symbolism resonates with my awareness of the consequences of suppressing true emotions or concerns.

Overall, these dreams symbolize a deep exploration of identity, guilt, and the dissonance between public personas and private realities. They reflect my introspection on past actions, cultural identity, and the consequences of silence or compliance. My dreams seem to highlight a journey towards self-acceptance, the reconciliation of inner conflicts, and the acknowledgment of complex emotions that I have long suppressed.

Yours, etc., Mannie

Letter #19

A Dream

13th April 2022

Dear Adeena

I dreamt I was in a synagogue service, and I was using the wrong order of service. I forgot my words; stumbled to find the right order, found it and carried on. I feel relieved that as a lapsed attender of services, I still know my way around the service. I realised that belief and habit come from different parts of the self; and also that my present position is one of respecting tradition, although not necessarily following it in my daily life; and that not following the tradition is not a source of guilt for me at having broken the chain of continuity. The continuity could be maintained by others, and I could dip in and out at will, and feel comfortable in both - in and out.

This position is connected to my age and experience having travelled through time and allowed myself to be influenced by exposure to new and different ideas and finding my own position viz a viz. tribal affiliation, faith, obligation and personal wish. To be sure, there are huge intangible influences of Judaism that make me and keep me Jewish, and in a world of division and hatred, I would be identified as a Jew, and I would suffer the same discriminations and stereotypical biases against which I would fight vigorously to retain my Jewish identity. I feel proud of what Jews have achieved in the world for good, but I am also aware that there are Jewish crooks and swindlers, but the parts do not constitute the whole, they merely reflect aspects of it, making Jews just like other peoples who struggle with the forces of good and bad in themselves.

My dream I think reflects these two parts of myself - the part of me that identifies with the tradition, is pleased that I know how to navigate my way in it, and the part of me that has let go and forged an independent and autonomous self that suits me well. After many years struggle, I feel okay now about getting things wrong, making mistakes. I can live with them and learn from them, provided no one is hurt by them. People may be disappointed in me making mistakes but that is their issue and it's up to them to work out their disappointment with me and move on. After all, decisions I make about my life should no longer affect decisions they make about theirs.

In psychoanalytic terms, my dream can be seen as a representation of my internal conflict and resolution regarding my identity and relationship with Jewish tradition. The dream's setting—a synagogue service—implies a connection with cultural and religious roots, serving as a symbolic space where my conscious and unconscious thoughts about tradition and belief converge.

The act of using the wrong order of service and stumbling over words signifies a moment of anxiety or uncertainty. This mirrors my unconscious fear of not living up to the expectations associated with my cultural and religious heritage. However, my eventual relief upon finding the correct order suggests a resolution of this anxiety, indicating that despite being a "lapsed attender", I still possess an intrinsic connection to my heritage. This reflects a deeper understanding that my religious practices and beliefs are ingrained in my identity, even if I do not actively practice them.

My dream highlights a distinction between belief and habit, suggesting that these elements originate from different aspects of the self. In psychoanalytic terms, this could be seen as a division between the superego (moral and cultural expectations) and the ego (the conscious self that navigates reality). My realization that not following tradition does not evoke guilt suggests a reconciliation with the superego. I accept that my deviation from traditional practices does not equate to a moral failing, but rather a personal choice.

The notion of respecting tradition while not adhering strictly to it points to an integration of my conscious and unconscious mind. My acceptance of this position—comfort in both involvement and detachment—demonstrates, I think, a mature resolution of internal conflicts, a hallmark of ego strength. This integration allows me a balanced identity, accommodating both respect for tradition and personal autonomy.

Moreover, the reflection on my age and experience indicates a journey of self-discovery, where exposure to diverse ideas has shaped my individual position. This can be seen as an individuation process, where I forge a unique identity distinct from collective expectations.

My dream also addresses the broader context of Jewish identity, acknowledging both pride and critical awareness. The recognition of Jewish contributions and flaws alike reflects an acceptance of the complex, multifaceted nature of identity. My assertion that my choices should not affect others indicates a boundary-setting process, asserting personal agency and autonomy.

In summary, this dream encapsulates my journey toward self-acceptance, the integration of diverse influences, and the formation of a unique identity that harmonizes respect for tradition with personal freedom.

Your loving Grandfather, Mannie

Letter #20

A Dream

The "Bridge"

17th February 2024

Dear Adeena

I dream that I am charged by my tutor to research the definition of "bridge". The assignment must cover, I'm told, all aspects of 'bridge' and the results are expected to be delivered soon. I ponder the question, and I feel ill-equipped to manage the assignment. I struggle to think of sub-questions that would go into the investigation: what is a bridge? What is the meaning of a bridge - the real thing and the metaphor? Who should I ask? How should I explain my task? How can I make this a serious inquiry that would add to the sum of our knowledge?

I start by thinking of a bridge as communication or a road bridge that enables long journeys to be shortened; I think of language as a bridge to understanding, how language enables people to make their needs known and also as a means of building relationships.

My mind moves to the difficulties of creating bridges; how in reality they are relatively unstable structures, and I think of recent disastrous tragedies of bridges falling down, like the one in Turin, Italy, but also elsewhere. I also think of the military needs to construct bridges quickly and quietly so that the enemy can be approached from behind.

I think of the bridge in the mouth that holds teeth together, a device that counters a tendency for things to fall apart.

In the next scene in the dream, I am at a conference and an ebullient man near me stands up and declares that all medical decisions involve a moral choice. There are murmurings against this idea, and I ask myself what my position is. In the dream, I declare my agreement with the statement about moral choice on the grounds that for everyone who gets the medical intervention, there is someone who does not. The choices involve a moral take - is there a connection here to a "bridge" - how to hold two opposing forces together?

In the final part of the dream, I arrive at the home of a country family, and I ask if I can be put up. Do they remember me? I was their guest a few days earlier. The gentleman of the family regrets that there are no rooms available as other guests have arrived and I notice the table is set for a large number of guests for a celebratory meal. The gentleman kindly recommends another establishment nearby.

I think the dream and its different sections points to the struggle we all have in negotiating throughout our lives, the presence of opposites, and their points of contact (in the Jungian sense of the 'conjunctio'), put broadly as our conscious lives of agency, wish and our purposeful drives for goals, and our unconscious selves - the hidden feelings of fear, shame and guilt that we prefer to bury. The "bridge" must surely also stand for the links between those two worlds - our inner and outer worlds. The "bridge" enables us to know both aspects - the highs and the lows, how drives and their frustration, our experience of self as unique individuals and as members of families and groups and society involving responsibilities and obligations, and therefore a degree of suppression of our individuality and instinctual drives.

This dream appears to explore complex themes of connection, communication, and the integration of opposites, using the metaphor of a "bridge" to represent these ideas. The dream can be interpreted as an exploration of my internal struggles and the quest for understanding and integration of different aspects of my 'self' and my external world.

The dream begins with a task assigned by a tutor, which suggests an authority figure or perhaps my own superego, pushing me to explore and define the concept of a "bridge." This task, I think, represents the pursuit of knowledge and understanding. My initial feelings of being ill-equipped point to a potential lack of confidence or an acknowledgment of the complexity of the task. This struggle reflects a deeper internal conflict or a challenge in bridging different aspects of my inner world (my psyche).

As I ponder the question, the metaphor of the bridge evolves. Initially, it symbolizes communication and connection, such as road bridges shortening journeys or language bridging gaps in understanding. This can be interpreted as my recognition of the importance of communication and relationships in forming connections with others and the external world. The reference to the instability of bridges and disasters, like the Turin tragedy, suggests an awareness of the fragility of these connections and the potential for breakdowns, both literally and metaphorically.

The mention of military bridges and dental bridges introduces the idea of creating stability in challenging situations. Military bridges symbolize strategic actions taken under pressure, perhaps reflecting my adaptive strategies in dealing with life's challenges. The dental bridge, which prevents things from falling apart, can be seen as a metaphor for my efforts to maintain personal and interpersonal stability.

The scene at the conference, where a man declares that all medical decisions involve moral choices, brings in the theme of ethical dilemmas and the tension between opposing forces. My agreement with the statement suggests an acknowledgment of the inherent moral complexities in decisions, reflecting an internal dialogue about values and ethics. The connection to the "bridge" here can symbolize the need to navigate these moral terrains, balancing conflicting needs and choices.

In the final part of the dream, I seek hospitality but find no room available. This scenario could suggest feelings of exclusion or a sense of not fitting in, possibly linked to my quest for belonging and acceptance. The gentleman's recommendation of another establishment suggests an acknowledgment of alternative paths or solutions, indicating resilience and adaptability.

The dream aligns with the Jungian concept of the 'conjunctio', or the union of opposites. The bridge serves as a powerful symbol of the connection between conscious and unconscious aspects of the self, the integration of personal desires with social responsibilities, and the reconciliation of individuality with collective norms. This integration process involves acknowledging and managing the dualities in life, such as success and failure, inclusion and exclusion, and moral dilemmas.

In summary, the dream reflects my internal exploration of complex and often conflicting aspects of life. The bridge symbolizes the journey of integrating these elements, emphasizing the importance of connection, communication, and balance in navigating my inner and outer worlds.

Your loving Grandfather, Mannie

Section 5
Societal Challenges

Letter #21

Society

3rd December 2021

Dear Shanan, Yoram & Danny

I am interested in the development of the differences in attitudes of people and how in some cases, these differences can be reconciled and in others they seem to lead to conflict and unhappiness. This was evident in my family and in other families, and as I grew up, I saw that happening in work groups and in the wider society. The most obvious conflicts in social attitudes and in formal social structures in South Africa, were around race relations. I was a member of the privileged white group, but I was also a member of the despised, rejected Jewish group. Balancing these conflicts in both aspects of my identity was problematic – when was I one and when was I the other? It created schizoid feelings me, walking a tightrope of identities in neither of which I could feel totally comfortable. Another question which I discovered in my analysis was how much of the social confusions stood for a more personal one, i.e. to what extent was I using the split in the social structures around me of race, religion, ethnicity and culture to project my own fears, hatreds, idealisations and quest for neatness, order and security. Whenever I returned to South Africa to visit my ageing parents, I noticed how easy it was to put my head in the sand and suspend the liberal ideals I had absorbed in England and sink back comfortably into the black/white and Jew/non-Jew dichotomies.

What was it about engaging with English liberal traditions that attracted me? Whatever else was lacking in British society, I was impressed by the abilities of people in conversation, in meetings and writings, to capture both sides of an argument, and the conviction that once the arguments had been presented, people should be free to make up their own minds. I found that a wonderfully refreshing and freeing process of thinking and tolerance and it felt like something I had been looking for all my life, enabling me to get away from the limiting either/or, good/bad, rich/poor, black/white judgements I so frequently heard in my family and in South African society – the pressure to make choices between limited alternatives. While still a young adolescent, I finally made the choice, and it was religious Zionist socialism in the form of collective living on a kibbutz in Israel.

My journey through various social contexts revealed the complexities of navigating conflicting identities and attitudes. Growing up in South Africa and later engaging with English liberal traditions highlighted the dichotomies in race, religion, and class, often mirroring my inner conflicts. The British emphasis on open dialogue and tolerance offered a liberating alternative to the rigid binaries I had experienced growing up in South Africa. Ultimately, I sought solace in religious Zionist socialism, embracing a more inclusive and nuanced perspective, but I ended up a student of Great Britain's great liberal democratic traditions and emboldened by my British psychoanalytic experiences. These influences did not erase the contradictions I carried but rather gave me the tools to hold them with greater awareness and compassion. They allowed me to move beyond inherited identities toward a more reflective, integrated self.

Yours loving Dad, Mannie

Letter #22

Kibbutz (1958) – An Experiment in Social Living

10ᵗʰ December 2021

Dear Shanan, Yoram & Danny

In my 18th year, I had the unique opportunity to live and work on Kibbutz Yavne as part of the requirements for entering the Hebrew University to pursue a B.Sc. degree in agriculture. This experience profoundly shaped my understanding of collective living and the complexities of community life. Kibbutz Yavne, a religious Zionist socialist commune, offered a blend of idealism and pragmatism that resonated with my own aspirations and beliefs.

The year-long experience was structured around a rotation through various agricultural fields. For four weeks at a time, I worked in different sectors, including orchards, incubators, chicken runs, banana plantations, ploughing, irrigation, cotton, vineyards, vegetables, landscaping, and spraying. This comprehensive exposure not only provided practical skills in diverse agricultural practices but also allowed me to experience the physical demands and rewards of farming. The summer heat often made the work exhausting, yet the sense of productivity and the tangible outcomes of our labour brought immense satisfaction.

The sense of camaraderie among the kibbutz members was one of the most fulfilling aspects of my time there. The communal lifestyle fostered strong bonds and a collective spirit. Working alongside others who shared a common goal created a supportive environment where everyone contributed to the community's well-being. Meals were shared, leisure time was communal, and there was a strong emphasis on collective decision-making. This environment fulfilled my pursuit of a more meaningful and cooperative way of life, contrasting sharply with the individualistic culture I had previously encountered.

However, my experience was not without challenges. Living in such close quarters with others revealed the complexities and difficulties of communal life. The intensity of daily interactions sometimes led to petty rivalries, gossip, and the formation of cliques and hierarchies. While the kibbutz aimed to minimize social stratification, subtle power dynamics still emerged, influenced by factors such as seniority, personality, and contribution to the community. These issues underscored the inherent challenges in maintaining egalitarian ideals within any human society.

Moreover, the kibbutz faced practical challenges in sustaining itself as an autonomous unit. While the community aspired to self-sufficiency, it was inevitably intertwined with the larger society. Economic realities required interactions with external markets, and cultural influences from the broader Israeli society seeped into the kibbutz, shaping its norms and values. This interplay between the kibbutz and the external world highlighted the limitations of attempting to create a completely independent and self-contained community. The kibbutz's economy was particularly vulnerable to fluctuations in agricultural markets and the broader Israeli economy. This dependence on external factors sometimes conflicted with the community's ideals of self-reliance and socialist principles.

Despite these challenges, my time on Kibbutz Yavne was an invaluable experience that broadened my perspective on collective living. It demonstrated the potential for creating a supportive and cooperative community while also revealing the complexities and compromises inherent in such an endeavour. The kibbutz model, with its emphasis on shared responsibilities and collective decision-making, offered a counterpoint to the more hierarchical and individualistic structures I had previously known. Yet, it also served as a reminder that no community, however idealistic, is immune to the realities of human nature and external influences.

My year on Kibbutz Yavne was a formative period that provided deep insights into the possibilities and limitations of collective living. The experience was a microcosm of broader societal dynamics, reflecting both the strengths and weaknesses of communal ideologies. While the kibbutz life was not perfect, it offered a valuable alternative to conventional living arrangements, one that emphasized cooperation, mutual support, and a shared vision. This year of practical work and social engagement laid the foundation for my studies in agriculture and continued to influence my views on community and society long after I left the kibbutz.

Your loving Dad, Mannie

Letter #23
Politics (1960s – 1970s)

22nd December 2021

Dear Shanan, Yoram & Danny

There were other groupings of white activists that existed outside the formal political frameworks that advocated for radical political change, even revolution. There was the South African Communist Party (SACP) which was founded in 1921 and tactically dissolved itself in 1950 after being declared illegal by the governing National Party under the Suppression of Communism Act, 1950. The Communist Party was reconstituted underground and re-launched as the SACP in 1953, participating in the struggle to end the apartheid system. Today it is a member of the ruling Tripartite Alliance alongside the African National Congress and the Congress of South African Trade Unions (COSATU) and through this it influences the South African government. The term 'suppression' in the name of the legislation, characterised much of life, culture and relationships in South Africa. Suppression was a psychological and behavioural theme in politics, education and religion and therefore in my personality development. Ideas of creativity, growth and expansion were restricted to commercial and manufacturing enterprises and most of my friends at school were products of this national and cultural belief system that led many of them into business or the money-making professions. They believed they had a right to the good life, they had money and all the accoutrements of a successful capitalist society and the accompanying attitudes. I, on the other hand, while also having the opportunities presented by privilege, chose another path – religious socialist Zionism with a hugely obsessive focus on the dream of Israel as the new Jewish Homeland that was established in 1947/48. I felt somewhat estranged from my frivolous, hedonistic friends for whom the seeking after pleasure seemed to play a central role in their lives, the egoistic pursuit of short-term gratification by indulging in sensory pleasures without regard for the consequences. I identified with the underdog, the dispossessed, disenfranchised, the poor and the broken and I believed in a delusional, unrealistic, superhuman way that I had the powers to change their situations, a conviction that partly sustained me in my drive to become a social worker (University of the Witwatersrand, 1961-64), then a psychiatric social worker (London School of Economics, 1967/8), then a psychotherapist (Tavistock Clinic, 1971-1975) and then an organisational and change consultant (Tavistock Institute of Human Relations, 1997 to the present). I also came to realise that these attitudes and motivations served hugely as a defence against recognising my inner conflicts over my relative inadequacies, helplessness and powerlessness and lack of status; the incorporated sense of inferiority that comes from a mix of Jewish persecution, a family culture of arrogance and distinction, and contempt for others outside the lager, and the struggle to find my sense of pride and a role. In other words, I was prone towards omnipotent and omniscient thinking, relished the phantasies of greatness and heroism that would come from changing society and the world. My wrong-headed narcissism knew no bounds, although I was careful to hide it by appearing to fit in with the prevailing culture, which I think I was, chameleon-like, quite good at. All this absurd psychic make-up was challenged in my psychoanalysis and my professional trainings that taught me about humility, facing disappointment, respecting boundaries – my own and others – acknowledging my limitations and the development of a tougher sense of realism about what is achievable and what is not and the ability to live with it. I spent 10 years on the couch fighting my psychoanalyst against giving up convictions about my specialness and learning to adopt a greater sense of just plain ordinariness. To be sure, it was also a tremendous relief to be able to give up my unsustainable, shaky self-image of great importance and consequence, and adopt the monotony of normality that allowed others in my life, like you, to have the space to breathe. I recall often in my work with groups thinking that usually when people speak in groups, on average they take, and are given about two minutes to speak. Longer than that, the group members get restless as if they feel that something is being taken from them. It is as if the person who hogs the conversation is 'stealing' something from the others, and soon enough, efforts start being made to shut down the offending 'theft'. Similar dynamics occur in families, in teams, in gatherings and in politics. I am sensitive to the tension between wanting all participants to have an effective voice in a group, and tendencies for undue domination by one or more members that result in the silencing of the majority. I see this in the tensions between liberal developmental democracies, on the one hand, and the cruel, sadistic authoritarian suppressed societies on the other.

"There is nothing so practical as a good theory"

"The best way to understand something is to try to change it."

These two famous statements, credited to Kurt Lewin, epitomize the idea of moving theory to practice and practice to theory. Lewin's provocative statements recognize the fact that our psychosocial reality, as human beings, has an inherent order and purpose to it. Lewin's dictum rests on the assumption that good theories are available to address practical problems. Conversely, there are bad theories to which people are sometimes dogmatically committed without supporting evidence. In research, imagination must focus on explaining why an effect may have occurred. Good theory can be highly practical, but it requires research designed to build and test theory or to evaluate the efficacy of theory-inspired interventions to real world problems.

The seven criteria for theory evaluation are scope, logical consistency, parsimony, utility, testability, heurism (the educational principle of acquiring knowledge through empirical study and practical experience) and test of time.

Although I have judged my mother to be a frightened woman with a suspicious nature, given to observing strict rules and the avoidance of fun, I wonder if that is the total picture. For I remember, during my early childhood, exploring the neighbourhood with friends, organising work parties to do gardening at my house, playing games, showing off and getting into mischief. Where did this spirited child get his drive from to venture out? I remember one day, I was about 4 or 5, I got it into my head that my father would welcome me and my friend shovelling a mud puddle through his car window onto the driver's seat. When he came out from lunch to return to work, he was so furious at what I had done, he gave me a walloping. I could not understand why he was so cross with me. What theory was I testing? How come I thought that my actions were a good thing and would be approved of by the person who would be discomforted and vexed by what I had done? Was my sense of reality disturbed, influenced by my desire for grandiose achievement that whatever I did would undoubtedly appeal to an appreciative audience? Or was there something more sinister and aggressive lurking in my mind towards my father about him being alone in the house with my mother, or was it about him being about to leave me alone with my mother for the rest of the afternoon while he was at work? As a 4- or 5-year-old, I doubt whether I would have been able to articulate such thoughts and feelings, but how else do I explain this splashy, muddy attack on my father and thinking it was a good idea? It seems extremely perverse behaviour, to persist with an action that would ultimately lead to my humiliation in front of my friend. Or was I showing off to my friend and wanting to be the heroic perpetrator of valiant deeds. I had wiped from my mind any thoughts of the consequences of my actions.

I think this type of rebellious behaviour, the search to be a somebody, continued into my later childhood and adolescence. I was driven to claim and display my unique identity as a kind of automatic reaction to my mother's strenuous attempts to control it. Part of my opposition was against her perceptions of her family, the Millers of Oudtshoorn, whom she praised and admired at every opportunity for their dignity and upstanding nature, and their renown as the pious family in the town. The 6 sons and 3 daughters of my grandparents were either businessmen or married to businessmen, but the grandchildren were in the main either doctors or other professionals. More than that, the family represented a much-admired unbroken chain of religious observance, not just from 'der heim' in Lithuania, but keeping the 'light burning' for and linking to many past generations stretching back into history. Much later, I was to discover that the shiny gloss of this family image was a mirage. Emigration from the threats and poverty in Lithuania had scattered the family, and scratching beneath the surface idealisation, one discovered rivalry and conflict between the siblings and very little credible love, warmth and support that one could get hold of and bask in. A family could talk up its greatness like a balloon, but it was just as easily pricked. Silence was a weapon used frequently and some members of the family, like my father and his brother-in-law, did not speak to each other over a business deal that went wrong for over 30 years right up to their deaths.

I have noticed I do something similar. When I have been crossed by a friend or colleague which is quite common in my field of work, I shut down on them, despite being aware that the people who make one angry represent a denied part of oneself, and that to heal the rift, one needs to face and talk to the 'enemy', to forgive. But I don't. I wipe that person from my consciousness and tell myself that the ideal of peace with everyone is an unattainable goal. Some people are just trouble, and it is best to steer clear of them, despite knowing that when I do this, I am 'splitting', which is regarded as an unhealthy state of mind. But there is madness in the world, represented by some people more than others. I am influenced by Gordon Lawrence, one of my supervisors/consultants who said that 'when you see a projection coming your way, stamp on it', separating this from projections observed in professional practice which are normally interpreted to provide insight to the 'projector'. Outside the professional role, projections may need to be suppressed. Gordon had many enemies whom he consigned to oblivion. But his statement eased my guilt when, in my role as a psychiatric social worker, I was obliged to remove children from their parents or incarcerate psychiatric patients or offenders and remove their human rights. I have no doubt that this type of work represented my symbolic efforts to deal with my own family by 'silencing' them, sending them away, denying them rights, in much the same way I believe was done to me. Troublesome and cheeky? Send him away. Strap him up in religious obligations, fears and prohibitions.

My narrative delves into the complexities of navigating identity, political engagement, and personal growth. I have reflected on the dichotomy between my privileged white status and marginalized Jewish identity in apartheid-era South Africa. My journey led me through various ideological paths, from religious socialist Zionism to psychoanalysis and professional roles in social work and psychotherapy. The exploration of inner conflicts, familial influences, and the impact of societal norms revealed a deep-seated struggle between my grandiose aspirations and a desire for normalcy. My story underscores the tension between idealism and reality, highlighting the challenges of balancing personal convictions with humility and acceptance. Through this introspective journey, I grapple with notions of power, responsibility, and the limits of influence, ultimately seeking a more grounded understanding of myself and the world.

Yours, lovingly, Mannie

Letter #24

Two Films

"Retablo"

"The Tinder Swindler"

23rd January 2022

Dear Shanan, Yoram & Danny

A Peruvian film director in one of my groups, Álvaro Delgado-Aparicio, invited the group to see his film *'Retablo'*. The story takes place in a remote Peruvian Indian community in the Andes, deeply religious in a stifling way, conservative and a form of strict social control; but the young adolescents in the town are crude, sexual, violent and sometimes out of control. The central story of the film is the relationship between an artist father and his adolescent son who helps him in his artistry making Retablos – painted cabinets that contain figurines of family groups, and other collections of groups of people, sometime religious figures for the Church. They are powerful religious symbols for ordinary people and many of the town's wealthy people commission the artist to create retablos for them, the church, etc. Life is hard, the community struggles to eke out a living on the harsh slopes of the mountain with sheep, cows, pigs and cotton. The family's living quarters are simple, primitive stone constructions, standing side by side with the barns of the animals. The opening scene shows the father training his son to see and remember the characters of a family standing together as if having a photo taken, so that back in their hut that serves as a studio, he will remember the characteristics of up to 20 people, young and old, male and female, their attire, their hair styles and distinguishing features. Back in the studio, the boy helps his father by kneading a thick potato mix for the figurines, while father paints bright symmetrical shapes on to the retablo. The relationship between father and son is of a wondrous all-embracing care and love and at this point I felt moved and frightened because of a premonition that something was going to happen to destroy the relationship.

"Retablo," is a poignant exploration of the tensions between tradition and individuality within a secluded Peruvian Indian community. The film deftly portrays the intricate and intimate bond between an artist father and his adolescent son, whose shared craft of creating retablos—decorative, figurine-filled cabinets with significant cultural and religious importance—serves as both a literal and symbolic medium of expression. The artistry involved in the retablos, meticulously captured in the film, reflects the vibrant yet restrictive culture of the community, where religious and social norms govern every aspect of life.

The film's setting in the Andean mountains is both breathtaking and oppressive, highlighting the harshness of the landscape that mirrors the community's rigid societal structures. Delgado-Aparicio uses this backdrop to delve into themes of identity, sexuality, and societal expectations. The portrayal of the town's youth as crude and uncontrollable contrasts sharply with the stern, conservative adult population, emphasizing the clash between burgeoning individual desires and the suffocating weight of tradition.

The narrative takes a dark turn as the son's discovery of his father's secret homosexual relationship shatters their seemingly idyllic relationship and the boy's perception of his father. This revelation is a turning point in the film, exposing the brutal reality of a community intolerant of difference and reinforcing the theme of suppression prevalent throughout. The father's subsequent ostracization and the family's descent into social isolation highlight the destructive power of cultural and religious dogma, as well as the painful consequences of living inauthentically.

"Retablo" is a masterful examination of the complexities of love, identity, and tradition within a tight knit community. The film poignantly captures the beauty of a father's love for his son and the devastating impact of societal prejudice. It serves as a powerful commentary on the dangers of rigid cultural norms and the suppression of personal truths. Through its compelling narrative and rich visual storytelling, "Retablo" challenges viewers to confront the consequences of intolerance and the universal struggle for acceptance and self-expression. The film's exploration of these themes resonates deeply, offering a nuanced perspective on the often painful path to self-discovery and the courage required to live authentically in the face of societal judgment.

The Tinder Swindler – film

The Netflix documentary "The Tinder Swindler" delves into the dark and perplexing world of Simon Leviev, born Shimon Hayut, a conman who posed as the son of a wealthy diamond magnate to defraud women across Europe. Leviev's manipulative tactics and fraudulent schemes have sparked numerous troubling reflections, particularly regarding his background as a Jewish Israeli and the son of a rabbi from Bnei Brak, an ultra-orthodox suburb of Tel Aviv. This piece explores the complex interplay between religious upbringing, societal norms, and the exploitation of human vulnerability that Leviev's actions highlight.

Leviev's background as the son of a rabbi is particularly jarring, given the stark contrast between his religious upbringing and his criminal actions. Bnei Brak is known for its strict adherence to Jewish law and the values of piety, humility, and community service. In this context, the notion that someone from such a background could become a notorious scam artist raises uncomfortable questions. Leviev's mother, appearing distraught in the documentary, ultimately disowns him, unable to reconcile his actions with the values she likely sought to instil in him. This public disavowal underscores the profound sense of betrayal and shame his family and community must feel.

One of the most disturbing aspects of Leviev's scams is his apparent understanding and manipulation of the concepts of belief and trust. Within many religious communities, including ultra-orthodox Jewish circles, there is a strong emphasis on faith and giving, often expressed through charitable donations. Leviev seems to have twisted these values to suit his nefarious purposes. He exploited the credulity and generosity of his victims, convincing them to part with their money under the guise of helping him escape dangerous situations fabricated by him. This mirrors, in a twisted fashion, the way some religious leaders might appeal to their followers' faith and goodwill for charitable causes. Leviev's actions, however, were not in the name of any higher purpose but purely for his self-aggrandizement and indulgence in a luxurious lifestyle.

The women Leviev targeted all shared a common dream of finding "perfect love." They recounted how he painted a picture of a fairytale romance, only to reveal fabricated threats from supposed enemies that left them feeling compelled to protect him. This narrative, combined with the illusion of wealth and power, created an intoxicating mix that clouded their judgment. It is a testament to the persuasive power of hope and desire; these women believed they were part of something extraordinary, even as they were being manipulated. The yearning for love and connection is a deeply human experience, and Leviev exploited this universal longing in the most cynical way.

The juxtaposition of Leviev's ultra-orthodox background with his actions as a swindler also raises questions about the influence of religious upbringing on ethical and moral development. While it would be unfair to generalize or stigmatize a community based on the actions of one individual, Leviev's case does highlight the complexities of human behaviour. His story suggests that religious upbringing, no matter how strict or pious, does not automatically safeguard against immoral behaviour. Instead, it underscores the importance of personal responsibility and the potential for any set of beliefs to be misused.

"The Tinder Swindler" ultimately serves as a cautionary tale about the dangers of blind faith and the importance of critical thinking. Leviev's victims were not only deceived by his charming persona and fabricated stories but also by their own desires and dreams. The film challenges viewers to consider how easily one can be led astray by appearances and the promises of an idealized life. It also prompts a deeper reflection on the vulnerabilities inherent in the human condition—our need for love, our susceptibility to manipulation, and the thin line between faith and folly.

Simon Leviev's story is a disturbing yet illuminating example of the complexities of human nature and the consequences of deception. His actions, set against the backdrop of his religious upbringing, challenge us to question our assumptions about morality, faith, and the power dynamics inherent in relationships. "The Tinder Swindler" not only exposes the dark side of online dating but also serves as a stark reminder of the need for vigilance and discernment in our quest for love and connection.

Your loving father, Mannie

Letter #25

Private Medical Insurance

2nd February 2022

Dear Shanan, Yoram & Danny

Today I am in a rage. All about private health insurance, which I have come to realise is irrational, anxiety-based, and unaffordable. For years we have been paying thousands of pounds in premiums, rising inexorably year-on-year, without any obvious benefits. We have an insurance broker who pushes us in the direction of renewing our policies for higher premiums. I checked with friends and learned they are paying between one-half and two-thirds less than us (!!) for similar cover. Is private health insurance purely a commercial transaction – you pay a premium; you receive health treatment and care, or is it a talisman designed to ward off psychotic anxieties about dying and death? Health insurance seems to be used as a safeguard against being lumped in with the general population, to avoid being just one among many, as in the thousands who must queue for services, and catering for the desire to be regarded as special, entitled and unique. All our working lives we have been paying our national insurance contributions from which funding for the NHS is drawn. We hear about the impossible rising costs of the NHS, about the ageing population and the effects of the pandemic, but these challenges must be and are being addressed politically. Private Health insurance seems to cater for wealthy expatriates, and it is advertised as luxury accommodation. What deception are the insurance companies carrying out and what self-deception do people like me collude with - that high premiums will give peace of mind – until you discover that one is being made a fool of. I have understood historically insurance was meant to cover the cost of a loss that one cannot afford to replace, like a house that burns down, or a ship that sinks. Overtime new 'insurance products' were created to cover more and more aspects of life. Average families usually cannot afford the cost of replacing smaller items, so why are we taken up by trying to recover the cost of everything through insuring them? My colleague, Burkard Sievers, thinks we are drawn to living the illusion of the perfect life with no flaws, no breaks, no illnesses and no disappearances that ultimately, at an unconscious level, is meant to prevent inevitable death – hence the anxiety around loss is a psychotic one that touches upon life itself. Dare I leave the house if I do not have health insurance? And what about the thousands and millions who do not have homes? Is insurance for them even an issue they can contemplate? The thought of it makes me anxious and overwhelmed by the enormity of the human problem of unequal or unfair distribution of the necessary resources to sustain life. Maybe I should relax more and be willing to face the risks and the unknowns of life without having an insurance policy against all ills. It seems insurance has replaced religion with the idea that performing certain rituals regularly, like the payment of a sum of money, will provide protection from divine wrath.

My medical health insurance is due for renewal in March and the annual increase is 30%; if next year's increase will be 30% again, that will take my annual premiums to £30,000, back to where we were a few years ago. Is it wrong-headed of us to bankrupt ourselves, so that the insurance will pay a fraction of our medical costs? What are we expecting and what are we buying? It seems insurance is about maintaining a certain privileged lifestyle, and not adjusting to realities of our circumstances. There may be a lot wrong with the NHS, but the care I'm getting is excellent, clean and efficient.

I am so furious about this thievery, and I must ask where this anger comes from. I think it comes from the feelings of helplessness, of being trapped in a monolithic, impersonal system that algorithmically determines how much I should pay and leaves me no choice in the matter, or if there is any choice it is about whether I want to cover this procedure or that procedure. It automatically extracts funds from me, and I am incapable of stopping it. Almost like the lifeblood draining from me while I watch it disappearing. The illusion I have bought into is that I am special and entitled to be treated as well as my wealthy friends, maintain the living standards of the upper class, to walk into pristine surroundings and to be made a fuss of and pampered. Private medicine in my view does not add to the general quantity of social good, it satisfies the whims and pretensions of people that need narratives to talk about at meals together, to declare triumphantly how magnificently they have been treated, how superior their service has been, how it saved their lives, as if the NHS could not have done so. Superior service for superior people. The pride and arrogance of this is sickening - a whole swathe of private medical care designed to feed greed, narcissistic display and omnipotence – how awful. I once took Leonie to a vascular surgeon for an examination of a wound on her legs who is regarded as a top surgeon, a charming man with a sense of humour. But soon enough he was examining me and hinting that he could attend to my kidney problems, privately of course. It wasn't hard to resist his pressure, but I had to steel myself and declined his secretary's invitation to see him for a check-up. How I loathe the insidious approach to join the elites for special treatment. What is this? Some self-defeating impulse to deny myself privileges, to identify with the poor of the world, and mobilise them to agitate for universal health coverage, politically sanctioned and paid for by everybody? I am committed to social equality and despise unearned privilege. I worked for 25 years in the NHS, and I had a senior role in a professional charity, but I also do private work. How contradictory is that? And what about consulting to companies whose products offer illusory solutions that also damage the planet and promote criminal opportunities? By consulting to them aren't I too seeking elitist approval and wealth? And writing books for prestige and acclaim? I should remember what my analyst, a well-known author, who says writing is an urge to improve things, an expression of a creative part of myself which I am prone to deny and disparage.

I'm not writing from my unconscious. I should be more playful and imaginative with events, people, and write more extended descriptions of what I am observing and experiencing. It is as if in my writing, I'm trying to solve problems, improve things, make appointments and describe projects, all very practical, not expressing the dynamics, conflicts, fears that inhabit my inner world.

Private Health Insurance, continued

This is a second instalment in the drama of Private Healthcare insurance. I run a post-professional development programme on organisational consultancy for organisational change agents. There is a participant on the programme, R., who as lead HR director of a global Healthcare insurance company, sits on the corporate board, is accountable to the CEO and he is also a coach to the CEO. In describing his relationship with the CEO, the company's strategy and the work he is called upon to do, R. was articulate and business-like. A business plan he helped to develop included the amalgamation of 5 businesses in Europe and the Middle East into one integrated structure. This integration occurred just before the pandemic broke and one of its consequences was an increasing number of complaints by clients/patients, and an increasing number of clients/patients were deciding to leave the company, the collapse of the company's market share and the departure of many high talent individuals from the company. It is R's responsibility to bring these matters to the attention of the CEO and to help the CEO find solutions. R's question to the group was how to address these problems with the CEO in R's Lead HR role without compromising his coaching role with the CEO. The method used in the workshop involves R. asking one other member of the workshop to be his consultant for the purpose of the exercise, while the rest of the participants observe the pair in action. The consultant, A., asked questions and commented on R's conflict of roles and the difficulty of maintaining both roles which R. acknowledged to be the case. But further questioning shifted the focus onto the unsaid issues in the company, in particular, the CEO's prime interest in the 'bottom line', the stakeholder value, and seldom talked-about type and quality of service provided to claimants. When challenged, R. said the company's primary task was 'to make money' which fed the CEO's arrogance and contributed to his aggressive, bullying behaviour, insisting his strategies were the correct ones that had to followed strictly by everyone. R. felt he could not raise these issues in his coaching sessions with the CEO. A. asked R. who the

CEO reminded him of in his life. This shift of questioning troubled R., but he gamely continued and said his grandfather who brought him up. His grandfather was arrogant, thought he was always right, and R. felt his self-confidence was undermined, as a result. A. pressed on and asked R. 'if your grandfather was here, what would you like to tell him?' R. was moved by this, and at first, he could not understand how this line of questioning related to the difficulty he was having in challenging the CEO. The key piece of information that was exposed was that private health insurance is based on the unlikelihood of members claiming insurance. Insurance is based on the principle of the few claiming against the funds of the many with the main financial beneficiary being the company. This made me think of my situation - I was relieved that my suspicions had been confirmed that as a premium payer at the level I am paying, I am being exploited and I should organise my finances better and become self-paying for medical expenses. I am less furious now because a plan is emerging, and Leonie can also see the wisdom of it. The plan is we terminate our health insurance and place the amount of the premium of £1700 a month (£20,000 at 2021 rates, rising to £27,000 at 2022 rates – a 35% increase – and therefore probably rising to £36,000 in 2023) into a separate bank account and pay for any private medical bills from that account. I anticipate that by the end of the year we will have made a saving.

Reflecting on my journey with private health insurance, I conclude that it is a system built on irrational fears and a misguided belief in its necessity. The exorbitant premiums we've been paying have offered little tangible benefit, serving instead as a false comfort against the inevitabilities of life. This 'false comfort' masks itself as security, yet it offers no real control over illness or misfortune—only the illusion of preparedness. It soothes anxiety without addressing the deeper vulnerability we all share, distracting from the need for systemic solutions and genuine community care. The realization that we are being exploited, paying much more than necessary compared to others, has been a catalyst for a deeper introspection. The facade of exclusivity and superior service in private healthcare is an illusion that caters to a desire for distinction, perpetuating a system that feeds on our anxieties and vanity. My work in both the public and private sectors has exposed me to the inherent contradictions and moral dilemmas in pursuing a life of unearned privilege. This privilege—granted by birth, social connections, or inherited wealth—often insulates individuals from the struggles faced by the majority, fostering a distorted sense of entitlement and merit. It raises difficult questions about justice, responsibility, and the ethics of benefiting from systems one has not contributed to meaningfully. The workshop with R. and the revelations about the true nature of health insurance further strengthened my resolve. The industry thrives on the low likelihood of claims, benefiting the company far more than the policyholders. This understanding has led us to a practical solution: to cancel our health insurance and self-fund our medical expenses, a decision that promises financial prudence and peace of mind. By reallocating the money previously spent on premiums into a separate account, we anticipate significant savings, liberating ourselves from the cycle of exploitation. This shift not only aligns with my values of social equality but also represents a personal rebellion against a system that prioritizes profit over genuine care. Moving forward, I choose to embrace the uncertainties of life without the crutch of insurance, confident in the excellent care provided by the NHS and reassured by the newfound clarity and autonomy in managing our healthcare needs.

Your loving Dad, Mannie

Letter #26

Sex

24th April 2022

Dear Shanan, Yoram & Danny,

I've been wondering how to write to you about sex without sounding like a textbook or an awkward guest on a daytime talk show. But here goes. It's important, after all—sex is part of life. And while there's no shortage of advice columns offering techniques and tips, this isn't one of them. I want to write about the emotional undercurrents—the hidden, early roots of sexuality that shape us in quiet but powerful ways.

Let's start with babies. Odd place to begin, I know, but bear with me. Have you ever watched a newborn feeding? The way they latch on, eyes rolling back, little hands clutching, body going soft with pleasure—it's almost sacred. Sometimes you see them give a little shudder of contentment, like they've just had the best meal of their lives. And maybe they have.

What's happening in those moments is more than just nutrition. It's the beginnings of something bigger. The baby is learning about satisfaction, closeness, waiting, relief—and yes, even joy. These are early templates for intimacy. The physical sensations are intense, and they're wrapped in warmth, sound, scent, touch. It's not *sexual* in the grown-up sense, of course, but it's part of the same tree—just the roots, still hidden underground.

Then comes the other side of the cycle: the poop. (Yes, I'm going there.) A baby's face when they've had a good bowel movement is priceless—pure relief. Sometimes it's even offered up to the parent like a little gift. And early on, parents accept it as such: "Well done, love!

What a lovely nappy!" But fast-forward a couple of years, and the same offering is met with "Oh no, that's disgusting!" And suddenly, something once celebrated becomes a source of shame.

That shift—joy to revulsion—is part of a broader story. As children grow, their early physical pleasures get dressed up in rules, expectations, and taboos. The body is slowly turned into a battleground of "yes" and "no," "clean" and "dirty," "acceptable" and "unacceptable." We all go through it, usually without much conscious memory. But it leaves a mark.

Now, back to that baby and the mother (or whoever is feeding them). Their dance is delicate. When it goes well, it's a duet of trust and pleasure. But it can also get tangled—misread signals, frustration, exhaustion. Some feeds are like jazz; others are like a bad duet on karaoke night. And when things go wrong, the emotional fallout can stick around.

Some mothers report feeling surprising sensations while breastfeeding—not just in the heart, but lower down, too. This can come as a shock, especially if no one has warned them. But it's a reminder: we are wired for connection, and those wires run through the whole body, not just the brain or the heart.

Fathers, for their part, can sometimes feel a bit sidelined. That powerful mother-baby bond might stir up feelings they don't quite know what to do with—jealousy, fear, even resentment. "Will I ever get her attention again?" some might wonder, half-joking but not really. In response, they might try to rush the child toward independence, sometimes under the noble guise of "encouraging resilience," but possibly because they're a little uncomfortable with all that closeness.

And this is where things get tricky. That early intimacy between parent and child can become tinged with guilt, even shame. The joy of bodily connection gets mixed with embarrassment and taboo. What was once sacred becomes something we're told not to talk about—or even to feel.

Of course, not all children internalize the same messages. Some breeze through those early years, others stumble. But many will carry a subtle sense that their bodies—and their pleasures—are confusing, maybe even dangerous. By the time they reach the so-called "latency period" (roughly ages 5 to 11), a kind of quiet sets in. It's like the volume on sexual feelings gets turned down. Not gone—just muffled, as if the psyche itself knows it's not quite time yet.

Then puberty hits. The lights come back on, louder than before, and suddenly the teenager is trying to navigate an emotional theme park without a map. All the old feelings—pleasure, shame, excitement, fear—come rushing back, but now in unfamiliar costumes. The early scripts we learned as babies start whispering again, sometimes helpfully, sometimes confusingly.

So, what's the takeaway here? Maybe it's this: sex isn't just something that begins at puberty or with a first kiss. It's a thread that runs all the way back to the very beginning—to suckling, soothing, waiting, releasing. The emotional patterns we formed in infancy—feeling safe or unsafe, wanted or rejected, delighted or shamed—become the scaffolding for our adult experiences of intimacy.

None of this is to say we're doomed by our early years. But understanding where some of these patterns begin can help us loosen their grip. And maybe, just maybe, we can treat ourselves and each other with a little more kindness, a little less judgment.

So yes, this letter was about sex. But not the kind you find in magazines or watch on TV. It's about the kind that lives quietly in the background, shaping how we reach for connection and how we respond when someone reaches back.

With love (and a bit of a blush), Dad

Letter #27
Wrong-headedness in International Relations

15th May 2022

Dear Grandchildren

So far, this book describes "wrong-headedness" in individual people - me, my mother, etc, but 'wrong-headedness' can be applied to leaders of organisations and nations too. In this letter, I will write about political wrong-headedness, that in the case of large entities, like communities and nations, leads not only to 'bad things happening', but to catastrophe and tragedy that lasts for generations, gets embedded in the DNA of a people, and serves as a semi-permanent reminder of their misfortune, from which they are seldom able to escape.

The recent invasion of Ukraine by Russia is a case in point - the presence of 'wrong-headedness' on a grand scale that has led to the dismemberment of a neighbouring state, and I don't want to cause you worry, but for all we know, the start of World War III. Putin, the authoritarian leader of a totalitarian government got it into his head that the former glory of Russia should be re-established and extended to non-Russian countries that were once part of the Russian Empire. Any signs that Ukraine was orienting towards the West, such as wanting to join the EU and NATO, was perceived by Putin as a threat to the motherland of Russia. This delusion - first an individual one, then by propaganda, extending to the rest of Russian society, spread like a virus and was bought-into by millions of Russians, until it became an unchallengeable truth. Any opposition or questioning of this "truth", is punishable by up to 15 years in prison. So, slowly, the re-construction of the Russian economy after the fall of communism, the development of its people through education, productive work, prosperity and good health, gave way to an extraordinary national obsession about hostile, dangerous intentions of the West towards Mother Russia; turning a creative productive existence into narrow small-minded messianic garbage about 'saving the pure Mother Russia' through the use of powerful arms and nuclear warfare. The wrong-headed ideas just grew and grew until it became the lived reality of almost everyone, looking for and finding 'evidence' to support the delusion and then using that as a springboard for further illusion and preparation to defend, turning Russia into a backward, dispirited country with only one narrative. Totalitarianism is a wrong-headed philosophy that stifles and suppresses people and does not recognise that people are different and whose differences can be accommodated in the wider polity, for the benefit of everyone. Instead, fear, anxiety and threat dominate the national consciousness, and this national myth becomes almost impossible to shift. This delusional and over-blown state of mind of the nation-state cannot last and huge projective process are created that soon enough implode – the country's desire to be the most powerful force in the world (presumably, to compensate for the country's shame over its inherent weaknesses) is projected outwards, so that the "other"- in this case, the West, led by the USA and UK, are perceived as wanting to destroy Russia, leading Russia to feel it must protect itself by puffing up its self-image, and expanding the space it occupies. To achieve this dominion, the country feels it needs a strong leader - a messianic figure - to save it from destruction.

At the level of the nation, these ideas are called 'international relations', but are they any different from the little child who imagines all sorts of dreadful dragons and monsters 'out there' who want to harm it? These wrong-headed ideas in an adult individual would be diagnosed as a psychotic mental illness and the patient would be admitted to a psychiatric hospital, but in the case of states the psychotic delusion leads to war and destruction; it reinforces the wrong-headed ideas of the defeated - "You see! They really were out to get us!" thus setting the scene for the continuation of the wrong-headed belief until the next war, even if it takes two or three generations to germinate. Wrong-headedness may subside for a while, but it never fully goes away, and soon it starts rearing its head again. The unconscious remains buried within all of us, somewhere.

Religion, in many respects a wrong-headed idea too, plays its part in keeping the illusion alive. Any philosophy based on purity (another wrong-headed idea) ceases to address the presence of impurities, which are usually 'projected' into others. Often, the solution is presented as annihilating the 'other' (the devil), in order to maintain the illusion of continuing purity (paradise). One only needs to examine the many rules and restrictions in all religions that separate 'us' (the pure) from 'them' (the impure) and who need salvation provided by the religion. It is noteworthy that in the Russian/Ukraine conflict, how the Russian Orthodox Church, whose leader is an ex-KGB officer, claims that God is on its side and that the Russian people and army are doing God's work worthy of Divine blessing and redemption. Wrong-headedness and the suffering it unleashes, knows no bounds.

The concept of "wrong-headedness," explored in this book, extends beyond individual folly to the collective psyche of nations and organizations. The invasion of Ukraine by Russia exemplifies how delusional thinking can escalate to catastrophic proportions, leading to widespread tragedy and generational trauma. The authoritarianism of leaders like Putin, backed by a totalitarian regime, transforms a nation's misguided ideas into an unchallenged narrative, perpetuating a cycle of fear, paranoia, and aggression. This collective delusion not only stifles progress but also fosters an obsession with perceived enemies, often resulting in devastating destructive consequences.

The interplay of wrong-headedness with religious dogma further complicates this dynamic, as ideologies claiming purity often exacerbate the illusion of an existential threat from the "other." The Russian Orthodox Church's endorsement of the conflict as a divine mission highlights how religious institutions can amplify nationalistic fervour, cloaking violent actions in moral righteousness. This dangerous blend of political and religious wrong-headedness traps societies in a vicious cycle, reinforcing misguided beliefs and justifying ongoing aggression.

Ultimately, the persistence of wrong-headedness in both individuals and nations reveals a deep-seated vulnerability in the human condition. It underscores the importance of critical thinking, empathy, and the recognition of our shared humanity. As history has shown, unchecked delusions at any level—individual, organizational, or national—can lead to profound suffering. The challenge, therefore, lies in cultivating a more reflective and open-minded approach, capable of embracing diversity and limiting the destructive consequences of wrong-headed thinking.

Your loving grandfather, Mannie

Section 6

My Senior Years

Letter #28

Kidney failure and dialysis

9th May 2022

Dear Shanan, Yoram & Danny

You will not be surprised to know that since starting on a regime of thrice-weekly hospital-based kidney dialysis 4 months ago, I have been thinking about kidneys and the treatment of the disease.

Kidneys are a pair of internal organs one hardly knows about. They sit somewhere around your middle, at the back, one on each side. They operate as silent filters, doing their work of removing poisons out of your blood system without you noticing anything. Your kidneys also do other things like: (i) eliminate excess fluid that has accumulated in the body because the kidneys are no longer removing it effectively; (ii) remove acid produced by body cells; (iii) maintain a healthy balance of water, salts and minerals, such as sodium, calcium, phosphorus and potassium, in the blood; (v) release hormones that regulate blood pressure; (vi) produce vitamin D to promote strong bones.

There are a few things that can slowly damage your kidneys, like having a high salt diet or taking medication for blood pressure that are not kidney friendly. This too happens without you noticing.

The health of one's kidneys is measured via annual blood tests that reveal the levels of potassium, sodium and phosphorus in the blood. These blood tests measure the rate of reducing efficiency of your kidneys to filter these toxins out of your blood to pass as urine. Failure to remove these toxins means that over time your body gets poisoned from within, and if left unattended, results in death.

I often wonder about the connection between the health of one's insides, sometimes called innards, viscera or guts, and the state of one's mind. After all, the infant's reactions to the rumblings of hunger in its stomach are extreme and contribute to what is called the paranoid-schizoid position, which is a feeling of intense vulnerability that threatens the infants total being, raising in it the prospect of being attacked and ceasing to exist - hunger produces existential threats, which may lead to, or be the result of the death instinct, or both. We only have to consider at the social level, how starvation has become an instrument of social policy in the Russian-Ukrainian war to force a nation out of existence.

But back to the kidneys - those quiet filtration plants, whirring away in the background, outside of consciousness, except when we go to the toilet. As a matter of routine, people over 50 are encouraged to have an annual blood test. The blood test provides a General Filtration Rate (GFR), which is a percentage of the maximum filtering efficiency of your kidneys. Over the years, my GFR scores went down by about 10% every six or seven years until it reached 25% efficiency, when I was referred to the well-known Kidney and Urology Unit of the Royal Free Hospital in London. There my declining state of health was explained to me by the doctors, nursing staff, the kidney psychologist and the dietitian, in calm and thoughtful ways, in a pattern of meetings that increased in frequency over two to three years, as we 'watched' the GFR scores drop from 25% to 10%, and 'waited' for the symptoms of the disease to develop. 'Watch and wait' was done by the 'Low Clearance' team, i.e. the team working with patients whose kidneys were clearing their blood at low levels of efficiency.

The Low Clearance Team explained that I should start preparing myself for a form of treatment for my failing kidneys - either dialysis, of which there are two main kinds, or a kidney transplant. A transplant was quickly ruled out because of my age and because of other diseases in my abdomen area - prostate cancer and Crohn's disease. The two remaining options were peritoneal dialysis or haemodialysis. I opted for haemodialysis because that way, we hoped, would lead to the least disruption of my work routines. Furthermore, haemodialysis could more easily be done at home, which would further reduce disruption by running the dialysis in the evenings and weekends.

You will notice how these remarks suggest that initially, I hoped my life would continue as before with only minor inconveniences. While this is true for most activity, the disruptions have increased progressively to the point where I think I must consider making major adjustments to my life, even including retirement. I had not anticipated the extent of the tiredness I would feel after each dialysis session and on some occasions the feeling of unwellness and headache. The recovery period of each session lasts between 12 and 18 hours, in other words, two good sleeps and some exercise to get my limbs fully functioning again.

At 15% GFR efficiency, I was moved to the treatment team to be prepared for dialysis. This involved having a fistula created in my arm about five months before the start of treatment. A fistula is a connection between an artery and a vein that is intended to allow for an easier insertion of the needles for dialysis, and it takes several months for the newly created artery to grow to enable efficient needling. Needling is the insertion of two needles into the artery to set up the lines that, firstly, direct my blood to the dialyser machine, and secondly, return the clean blood to my body.

Now, from the mechanics and structures of the treatment to its impact on my emotions and thoughts, in other words, my state of mind. In my professional work, I frequently rely on the Tavistock Institute's concept of *socio-technical systems*, and I discovered that I and the dialyser act as one integrated socio-technical system involving me in a supine, patient role and the dialyser standing imperviously alongside me, rather like a robot out of Star Wars, buzzing, hissing and thumping bloodlines, jumping about in time to the thumping of the dialyser with occasional alarms going off, signifying something is wrong, like my venous and arterial pressures falling outside their limits, the needles lying in the wrong position, etc. As I have described before, my life is dependent on this machine, but I fail to take in the enormity of this situation and my part in the sociotechnical system in which I feel I'm only a bit player. The nursing staff on the ward are competent and humane and we have built personal relationships with them, talking about one another's families, and my anxieties about the treatment.

This week I was told I would have to attend the hospital for treatment three times a week, up from twice a week because of increased potassium levels in my blood. This came as a shock and I fell into a deep depression, thinking I now cannot avoid the implications of my disease and its treatment - they're both taking up a larger part of my life which means that I will have to give up some things and the blackest thought of all, that I am on my way to die, not helped, I must say, by the death two weeks ago of a 37-year-old patient, two beds away from me. These events made me wonder whether the reassurance I had received from the team that I could live for years on this regime, has any substance to it, or was simply false reassurance. This week I feel especially ill - massive headache all day on Wednesday, pains in my abdomen and chest, causing me to worry about whether I will have time to complete my writing projects. Speaking to my psychoanalyst about the situation and my feelings is a great help and it is making me braver in facing my end, while still taking up the challenges of living and using the opportunities I have. But the thought of me ceasing to exist, also makes me impatient to get things done quickly, for example, the trilogy I am writing with David: the final two volumes are nearly finished, but David keeps wanting to introduce more theories, interesting ideas and people that he picks up from his extensive reading, while I say we must consolidate, close the writing, and send the manuscript off to the publishers. I think my experience of time has become so different to the sense of time we both shared in the early stages of the writing, when time for both of us seemed to stretch indefinitely into the future - we were, after all, writing three books!

My journey through kidney disease and dialysis has been a profound and transformative experience. Initially, I approached the situation with a sense of hope and a desire to maintain my normal life with minimal disruption. However, the reality of the treatment and its side effects, such as fatigue and the psychological burden of dependence on a machine, has required me to reevaluate my expectations and make significant life adjustments. The psychological effects of dialysis have been particularly challenging, as they undermine my sense of identity and provoke existential reflections on mortality. The increasing frequency of treatments, the emotional toll, and the inevitable decline in health have forced me to confront the fragility of life and the urgency of completing my work.

The impact of my condition extends beyond myself, affecting Mum, you, my children, my grandchildren and my colleagues. They all grapple with the emotional strain and practical implications of my illness. The wrong-headed thinking in my past, such as not critically examining the long-term consequences of a high-salt diet or certain medications, contributed to my current situation. This realization emphasizes the importance of conscious, informed decision-making about one's health. As I continue to navigate this difficult path, I strive to balance the challenges of living with the reality of my condition, cherishing the time I have left and the opportunities still before me.

Living with kidney disease has become a profound and emotional journey, but it is my family—my wife Leonie, you, my children, and my grandchildren—who occupy my thoughts most. The looming fear of being absent from their lives, of missing their laughter, their achievements, and their simple daily joys, weighs heavily on me. I cannot shake the sense of loss I already feel, imagining the void my absence might create.

A constant undercurrent of guilt runs through my thoughts, particularly when I think of Leonie. Her life has been altered in ways I never wanted. Her desires, her dreams, and her needs seem to take second place to my illness. I worry that the responsibilities she has taken on, the sacrifices she continues to make, have overshadowed her own happiness. The idea that I am a burden, that my condition has curtailed her freedom, fills me with a guilt I cannot escape.

My children and grandchildren have also been touched by this change. I see the worry in their eyes, the extra care in their words. I fear that my illness has become a shadow over their lives, a constant reminder of fragility. I dread the possibility of being a source of their sadness or stress.

At times, I wonder how they will cope when I am no longer there. Will their lives be overshadowed by grief, or will they find strength in each other? I hope that my love, my words, and the memories we have created will be enough to sustain them. More than anything, I want them to know that, even in my absence, my love for them endures, and that every moment with them has been a gift beyond measure.

But beyond the sadness, I also feel gratitude. Gratitude for their unwavering support, their patience, and their love, which has given me strength in my darkest moments. I hope they remember the laughter we shared, the stories we told, and the love that wove us together, a love that not even distance or absence can diminish.

Yet, beneath all of this is a deep, aching sadness—a longing for the life I once had with Leonie and our children. I miss the simple, everyday moments—the quiet dinners, the laughter, the shared plans for the future that seemed so certain. That life now feels like a dream fading away, and I grieve its loss, even as I cling to the memories. And alongside this sadness, there is anger—anger at the unfairness of it all, at the relentless erosion of the life I loved and the joy I once shared with those closest to me.

Your loving Dad, Mannie

Letter #29

Kidney Dialysis

26th December 2021

Dear Shanan, Yoram & Danny

I am sorry to let you know that from today, I shall be a regular patient on kidney dialysis for the rest of my life, following the diagnosis of End Stage Kidney Disease some months ago. The kidney dialysis process begins at hospital with washing my hands and arms to create a sterile environment, going to the linen cupboard for the sheets, pillowcases and blanket, and making my bed. When that is done, I take various measurements and record them in my personal file. I weigh myself (71 kilos approx.), take my temperature (36.6 usually), measure my blood pressure (147/75 usually).

I then prepare the instruments to be used in the dialysis - protective sheets of green and white tissue paper (2), syringes (3); I tear off 10 strips of sticking tape that will hold the needles in place, swabs, the needles lines (3), disinfectant tissue. Tearing the items' protective wrappings off and laying them out, must be done without physically touching them to maintain their sterile state. I then have to 'line' the dialyzer, which involves inserting the outflow and inflow tubes (the lines) into the machine and connecting them to the dialyzer. It is complicated and I am anxious about making mistakes. It takes many attempts to get it right and I'm about three-quarters the way there. Nurses are always on hand to assist. When all the instruments have been laid out on the mobile table, when I have taken all my measurements and recorded them in my personal file, I am ready and I get into bed, make myself comfortable and wait for the nurse to come and needle me - two insertions, the red line for the outflow of blood and the blue line for the returning inflow.

Both needles are inserted on my right upper arm about 2-4 centimetres apart above the Fistula that was created near my elbow in July last year. The Fistula is interesting because it is the creation of a new channel in my circulation system by cutting one of the two arteries in my arm and connecting it to a smaller vein. Over time the smaller vein grows to resemble an over-sized artery, and it is into this enlarged arterial space that the needles are inserted and taped down. My right arm is meant to lie still on a pillow so that the needles do not touch the walls of the artery. If they do, either because they have not been inserted properly or because I have moved my arm, making the needles touch the artery wall, my blood pressure drops, the monitor starts beeping, and nurses rush over to correct the position. I may feel unwell as my brain is deprived of oxygen, so my bed is tilted back so that my head is lower than my legs, I take deep breaths until good oxygen levels are restored, and after about 30 minutes, we are on our way again.

I realise I have a growing and complex relationship with my dialyzer, the machine that purrs, and hiccoughs, quietly beside me, its circulating wheels, like 3 large buttons down the front of a jumper, or like a three-eyed monster, doing its work, rather impersonally, and mechanically, yet carrying the responsibility of ensuring I continue to live, but not really being "interested" in me in any other way. It has no feeling for the previous patient who used the machine and no anticipation of the patient who comes after me. Yet, if there is one small variation in the process - changes in blood pressures, changes in blood flow, pulse rate, the machine goes crazy, lights flashing, setting off alarms that can be heard throughout the ward and won't stop until somebody comes, taps the console screen, corrects the variables, and we, the machine and I, move on.

I discuss with the nurse attending me, Menges, my disheartening discovery from a blog on the internet that the dialyzer provides me with only between 5% and 10% of my kidney functioning. He is shocked to hear this claiming instead that it is closer to 60%. He scurries to his books or computer and comes back and says we are both right – the 5%-10% improvement refers to the average over the week; the 60% refers to improvement on the day of dialysis. In other words, the period between dialysis sessions sees a deteriorating efficiency of the kidneys, as the toxins and accumulating fluid clog the system again – c'est la vie, you win some; you lose some. We learn that calling dialysis a 'renal replacement therapy' is a misnomer. It seems that a machine, that was discovered 80 years ago in 1943 in war-torn Holland, by Dr Willem Kolff, a young physician, cannot fully replace the unique and exquisite functioning of the kidneys that have evolved and developed by nature over billions of years. The kidneys have 7 important functions - controlling acid-base balance, controlling water balance, maintaining electrolyte balance, removing toxins and waste products from the body, controlling blood pressure, producing the hormone erythropoietin, and activating vitamin D. One machine doing all that may seem miraculous; rates of efficiency would be variable – better on some of the factors, less well on others.

I have referred elsewhere of my growing interest in kidney disease research. It is natural that the big events in one's life would trigger an interest in knowing more about the subject, not just as a curiosity, but also linked to the possibility that the efforts of a research scientist may throw light on something new that could increase knowledge and improvements for other kidney disease sufferers. For the first few weeks of my dialysis, I was heavily focussed on the details of preparation and process of the dialysing to think about 'research', but later, a chance remark by my nurse that I seemed interested in the dialyzing process, prompted me to ask, 'well, isn't everyone here?' He replied that not everyone is interested in their dialysis, and that remark made me think of 'denial' as a response to threats to one's life, and the possibility that this could be the basis of a possible research project – how does denial – individual, family and professional – impact on the adoption of life-promoting kidney dialysis. A secondary thought was how could *socio-technical systems and design* and the *functioning of social systems as a defence against anxiety,* two major theoretical constructs coming out of the Tavistock Institute over the past century, could offer new perspectives on the disease and its treatment than more common traditional research methods. Moreover, as I now was part of a 'socio-technical system' of my very own (me and the dialyzer), and my anxieties about my disease and its treatment were high, I could use my own experiences to inform the research question and methodology. At the next meeting with my renal consultant, I put the question to her of researching patients' experience of dialysis and to my surprise she was immediately eager to take the discussion forward and offered support of the hospital and the department. I next wrote to my CEO, Eliat Aram, and from her too, there was immediate enthusiasm and excitement. At her suggestion, I wrote to my colleague in group relations, Rune Rønning, a researcher in Norway, who was formerly a dialysis patient, and he too was keen to make available resources in the health domain in Norway. I felt I was no longer alone in the drama of dialysis, but that things were coming together in a way that might expand the understanding of my experience of the interference in my line of life that I had got accustomed to during my adulthood. But that was not always so – since childhood I had had to adjust my life according to recurring illnesses such as asthma which had resulted in a massive dislocation of my life and no doubt on my personality development. I had generally thought of myself as a healthy person, coping reasonably with life's stresses and strains, but now I am having to re-evaluate that image and identity and ask myself whether illness had been mobilised by me to form a key part of my identity. I sometimes felt, even though I denied it to myself, that I had used illness and the patient role to join with and seek connection, as a 'special' person, with other special people - admired and idealised healers which was very much part of my family's culture, and undoubtedly, Jewish culture too. Seeking and receiving their attentions certainly fed into my victim identity and falsely offered me a sense of protection by being accepted into the folds of hallowed 'medical' company.

Today, I came for my dialysis session intending to photograph aspects of the preparation and process, but I only managed to get a few simple shots of the stationary dialyser and little of the process. It's difficult operating with one hand. I had wanted to video the needling to get better acquainted with the process, but first I must practice my camera technique! It's quite something to video yourself being operated on. I hoped that by doing so, I would overcome my anxiety and the pain when the time comes to self-administer the needles. The size of the needles increases over time, starting with small, progressing to medium and then to large. Now, I am on medium. The larger the size, the more painful. Today was difficult. I couldn't get the needle in properly, the blood clotted, and the needle had to be taken out and the process started again. Doubly painful. I don't know how I'm going to do it. The tea trolley comes round, and I had a welcome cup of tea and Leonie's wonderful sandwiches. The dialysis takes three hours, so there is plenty of time to read, do emails and eat, and sometimes sleep. Apart from the medical advantages of the treatment, I do actually look forward to going to hospital each time and being in a different environment and relating to different people. I have been asked to be interviewed by young medical students. I enjoy that because of the opportunities to teach them something about the whole person, and not only about symptoms. The consultant who organises the students is friendly, and he told me I'm a hit with them. They're a hit with me - young, eager, polite, wanting to learn more, so I get into telling them about *socio-technical systems* and *social systems as a defence against anxiety* approaches. I give them Isabel Menzies' paper on the subject.

Watching my blood clot today was frightening, an ugly red blob falling out of the needle. It happened so quickly. The nurse explained it sometimes happens when the fistula is not fully developed. That is why the Fistula is created 6 months before the start of dialysis. This may have been explained to me by the Low Clearance Team, but I don't remember.

Today, the needling was difficult. The first needle went in properly, but the second couldn't find the artery. It appears the fistula is undeveloped and zigzags in my arm making it easy to miss. Together, Nurses Marilyn and Faviola made three painful attempts to re-needle me. This caused my blood pressure to drop quickly making me to feel unwell and sweaty. Nurse Faviola worked on me for a long time, making sure I was comfortable, pain free and retaining reasonable blood pressure levels. I recall what my analyst said about the dialysis experience and its meaning. He supports the view of my dependency on the dialyzer echoing the mother-infant relationship with some of the struggles the baby has on latching onto the nipple; of contending with mother placing/feeding milk into it and fluids and waste removed by mother. His comment made me think about watching my blood leave my body and return – just seeing my blood outside of my body. This links to my depression, which I only cursorily dropped into the conversation with my analyst in a list of my 'exciting achievements' that have occurred since my last session 3 months ago. My murderous feelings towards my analyst were graphically expressed in a dream I had brought, because, he said, I did not want to offend him, like the baby fears offending its mother that may cause her to stop the feeding. I spoke about the writing Masterclass, how much I was enjoying it and regard it like psychoanalysis. Leonie had said that my anger about the private medical insurance was a displacement of my rage against my analyst for his long absence; probably true, I had a headache for the rest of the day and night. My medication has changed and that may be lowering my blood pressure too. In my dream, I allowed things to happen to me, sexual seduction with violence, because I was reluctant to offend. This appears to be the case regarding my feelings about the insurance issue which has run on for years without any serious questioning or reviewing the insurance system - payments and benefits. My depression is debilitating, painful and interferes with my life and relationships. I have yet to come to grips with the fact that my life is now permanently dependent on the dialyzer, the Machine.

In closing, my life now revolves around the reality of being a permanent kidney dialysis patient. The meticulous process of preparation, the anxiety of potential complications and the psychological impact have all become daily companions. The relationship with the dialyzer, this complex machine that sustains me, evokes a mix of gratitude and unease as it mirrors the delicate balance of my existence. The reality of only partially replacing my kidney functions with a machine underscores the limitations of technology and the irreplaceable intricacy of human organs. My recent reflections have led me to ponder the role of denial in coping with life-threatening illnesses, sparking a potential research interest. This exploration aligns with my work on socio-technical systems, and the support from colleagues and the hospital has been encouraging. My encounters with young medical students offer a fulfilling opportunity to share insights, emphasizing the importance of seeing patients as whole people. Despite the pain and challenges, there is a strange comfort in the routine of hospital visits and interactions with staff and other patients. Yet, the overarching truth remains: my dependency on this machine is a permanent fixture, a sobering reminder of the fragility of life and the inevitability of change.

Yours patiently, Dad

Letter #30

Kidney Dialysis

31ˢᵗ October 2022

Dear Shanan, Yoram, Danny and Adeena

At this moment, I am on a dialyser, having kidney dialysis. I have just "come on" and I'm proud and satisfied that I did the needling on my own without any hitches, like a 2-year old child who exclaims, "me do it; me do all of it". No nurse was in the room, and I even had a coy remark from my named nurse, "oh, so you didn't call me, I'm not needed anymore!" This new skill in self-care brings me a step nearer towards a more flexible lifestyle by moving the dialysis to home, called Home Haemodialysis - HHD for short. I still have a few hesitations when I "come off" the machine, but I hope today I will do that successfully. Arnel, my named nurse, is an accomplished teacher for letting patients experiment in going through the process themselves.

Today, I imported the data about myself into the dialyser's computer, and I think I have got the timing right – for the first 30 minutes, no fluid will be drawn off, and then at 30 minutes I change the computer to remove 900 millilitres in three hours. The first 30 minutes without fluid withdrawal are meant to allow my body to adjust to the dialysing to avoid my BP crashing that leaves me feeling unwell and approaching a faint.

I have just changed the fluid draw off to 900ml in three hours, and already I have started yawning, the first indication that my BP is dropping. I am hoping to remove 900ml because it means that I am likely to weigh quite a bit less at the end of the dialysis session/treatment. I'm also satisfied with the blood pressures - arterial at -115 and the venous at +145 - because it means that the needles have been inserted properly without touching the walls of the artery and vein. I've just had a light lunch of one sandwich, a cup of refreshingly hot tea, a biscuit and half an apple. Eating reduces blood pressure, which when added to a drop in my BP that happens naturally, may lead to an extreme crash of 90/50 and then I will be in trouble - so far there is no sign of a crash as I look up anxiously and scrutinise the BP readings on the computer screen. We're holding up and I'm praying that this will continue. I shall be out of the woods in about 30 minutes, with the remainder of the dialysis usually proceeding smoothly. I think I will even be able to sleep a little and that should help because sleeping involves lowering the back of the bed so that I will lie horizontally, with my head slightly below the level of my feet, and that helps bring my BP back to normal levels in about 15 minutes.

I have described the technical aspects of the dialysing, which, of course, are hugely important. I've had to learn the 60-odd steps in setting up the machine and getting myself ready for the needling to link up with the dialyser, and the 30-odd steps in coming off. But I also need to say something about the psychological, emotional aspects and the effect of a changing identity. All this, in addition to the impact of the dialysis on my daily life, my work, my sense of myself and what kind of joint future Mum and I will have.

The second round of tea is coming shortly, and I can have my second sandwich, biscuit and apple. I look forward to the second round of tea (which was later cut to save costs) because it means the treatment session is nearly over. After tea, I start preparing to come off - setting up the materials for removing the needles and patching myself up.

On the issue of identity, I sometimes ask myself how I got into this position of having end stage kidney disease. There is no history of kidney disease in my family so that should rule out any genetic predisposition. My mind turns to the blood pressure tablets I have been taking daily for the past 45 years approximately. I remember clearly how I attended St Mary's Hospital Hypertensive Unit while we experimented with various combinations of medication to control my high blood pressure. I never got to know how high my BP was or whether I could live with it. The tablets as far as I know were high in sodium, and taken together with my high salt diet, probably were the cause of the deterioration of my kidneys and making me one of the 3.5 million kidney patients in the UK.

Dialysis: Facts and Feelings

The three basic functions of dialysis are:

1. Removal of toxins in the blood that is no longer done efficiently by the kidneys.

2. Balancing the requisite levels of chemicals in the body like potassium, sodium and phosphates that is normally carried out by the kidneys.

3. Removal of excessive levels of fluid in the body, which is normally done by the kidneys.

This "removal" in all 3 points above is normally done through urinating, which is why most patients with End Stage Kidney Disease (ESKD) do not urinate. There are four or five other functions performed by the kidneys, but they do not concern us here. I am concerned with feelings and emotions associated with ESKD and kidney dialysis.

Firstly, kidney disease creeps up on people as there are no symptoms letting one know that they are unwell. Discovery of kidney disease is mainly by having regular blood tests and observing the Estimated Glomerula Filtration Rate (eGFR) score. An eGFR of 60 or higher is in the normal range, although the eGFR normally decreases with age. An eGFR of below 60 may mean kidney disease. An eGFR of 15 or lower may mean kidney failure.

In my case, I observed a gradual decrease in my eGFR from about the age of 65, dropping an average of about 10% every five years. Once it reached the 20% level, I was referred to the Royal Free Hospital (RFH) Kidney and Urology Department, which I attended for regular blood tests, medical checks, and advisory and planning meetings with nurses and dietitians at which we discussed the importance of maintaining a sodium free and potassium free diet, and detailed discussions with doctors and nurses about treatment options. The RFH also ran an information evening at which various treatments were demonstrated on machine models. Patients were also on hand to answer questions. The treatments on show were mainly home haemodialysis, and peritoneal dialysis, but also kidney transplant, for which I was not eligible for reasons of age and presence of a hernia.

It was slowly emerging that a huge sea-change to my lifestyle lay ahead, but I had little idea of just how large and disruptive the change was to be. I think I was in a state of emotional denial, thinking that my life would continue in roughly in the same way it was going then, perhaps with a few interruptions for appointments, here and there. Little did I know about the upheavals and dislocations that would be involved in trying to preserve as much as possible of my kidney functioning, while at the same time trying to preserve as much as possible of my family life and my work routines.

And here is a relevant thought that crosses my mind now, as I write, but not then. The physical functioning that I had taken for granted all my life without thought or consideration, can be said to come under the umbrella term of "filtration". Waste products that result from digestive processes and from cells in the body that grow, decay and die, are expelled in daily toilet routines which one hardly gives a second thought to, once one has left toddlerhood when toilet behaviour is a huge issue, and sometimes a source of tension between toddlers and their parents. When I practiced as a psychiatric social worker in the 1960s in child guidance clinics, I notice how children who were referred because of concerns about toilet habits, or had developed diseases of the bowel or bladder, tended to have fastidious, controlling mothers obsessed with neatness and tidiness and a preoccupation with getting things right, including strict rhythms of feeding, defecating and urinating, and sharply-focused attention on the foods eaten by the child.

And similarly, I could describe my professional practice as "filtration" a continuous thoughtfulness (filtering) in my mind whether the material presented by patients (and later, by my organisational clients) were real or fantasised accounts of their realities, despite being strongly and genuinely felt experiences, or were they projections or feelings that in their telling were meant to make me feel what they were feeling as a means of obtaining relief from inner conflicts. A "projected" feeling is a feeling that is expressed in the present that is accompanied by emotions that originate in the past. So, for example, if a patient complains that I appear to have no proper interest in them, I might think of the possibility that the patient was projecting into me, feelings of rejection they may have experienced in relation to parents, in their earlier lives. Or, if I find my mind is actually wandering away from the patient, I may ask myself if that might be evidence of the patient's projected anxiety of their fear of abandonment and I would say something like that to them.

Then in my work with organisations where environments and relationships may be impersonal, exploitative, and suffused with fears and resentments, listening to the stories of the people would also involve a high level of filtration, syphoning out the toxicities in the stories from the realities of work and organisational life with its stresses, competitiveness, climbing the promotion letter, and so on.

My professional efforts are aimed at distinguishing between layers of emotional experience and providing understanding of how individuals, and groups, can get caught up in the pressures of the systems in which they work. I feel a pressure to retain my independence of thought, not to get swept along by the patient's feelings, but to accept them non-judgmentally, which produces strain on me, particularly if the situation being described is very toxic, as they often are.

My contention is that there may be a correlation (not the same thing as causation) between the work one has chosen to do and the organs of one's body that eventually succumb to disease. I see a correlation between my professional role in "filtering" the elements of the client's story and the failure of my kidneys' filtration function.

In my profession, great emphasis is placed on having adequate support systems, which for me, includes personal psychoanalysis, numerous supervisions, long-term executive coaching, good managerial support, regular team meetings, academic study and attendance at professional development conferences, programmes, seminars, etc. Support systems are designed to 'filter' out the dynamics that belong to the self and those that belong to the patient/client. This filtration is an important part of keeping a realistic perspective and ability to understand deeply what the patient or client is experiencing dynamically without becoming overwhelmed by the patient's emotions or over-identified with the client's position. Failure to differentiate, which happens often, lessens one's capacity to help, and hence the need for support systems. William James, the American psychologist and philosopher who developed the notion of pluralism, wrote: *"to the very last, there are various "points of view" which the philosopher must distinguish in discussing the world".* (James, W. (1905). *The Will to Believe and Other Essays in Popular Philosophy*, pg. viii. University Press. Cambridge, USA)

But back to my current emotional state at this time of 3 x weekly dialysis for nearly 4 hours, which end- to-end, with travel, set-up and coming off, lasts 7 hours. It is easy to focus and describe the practical behaviours of administering the dialysis – washing my hands, preparing the supplies, making the bed, lining the dialyser, washing my fistula, needling, taping, adjusting the arterial and venous pressures, lying down and keeping an eye on the pressures on the computer screen, the blood flow rate and the volume of fluid removed, the re-infusion, the uncoupling from the machine and taping up without losing any blood. I have mastered all these steps - 60 steps for coming on and 30 steps were coming off - in preparation for doing the haemodialysis at home.

But what about the emotional impact of the diagnosis - what does it mean to me psychologically and to my identity? I cannot escape the big question that from now on my life depends on a relationship with a machine, which, in turn, makes me feel as though I am living on borrowed time, that I am a few steps before the grave, despite knowing that technically speaking, the treatment can keep me alive for several years. This depresses me greatly especially when I'm not busy, like on Sundays when I fall into a stuporous depression. I am not motivated to do any of the usual household or work chores; it is as if something outside my control makes me give up, withdraw and just stop. It is frighteningly different from my other self - focused on relationships with my wife, children and grandchildren, on work, being interested in achievements, writing and publishing, speaking well, attentive to legacy, and playing a responsible role as a public citizen. This attack on my identity is significant - it has shifted from being a well-trained and widely acknowledged as an experienced and effective psychotherapist, an international consultant, widely respected for the books I have written and the help I give to others to write, a loved husband, father and grandfather, to a sick old man. I fight against this label, and I avoid speaking about the diagnosis when we are with friends. A sense of isolation has developed as if I now represent not life, but death, making people want to keep away from me. To be sure, the pandemic and lockdown contributes to this feeling of shutting down and ending. I am acutely aware of this rapid approach of the end. I see the many patients in hospital who appear to have given up, just so many bodies helplessly tied to their dialyzers as their lifeblood flows out of them, and comes back "washed", as one doctor put it to me. The process does not appear to invigorate them, although some patients when I speak to them, liven up. I feel I have a mission to be lively, so I stride up and down the ward greeting nurses and patients, asking them how they are to liven things up a little, and I try to encourage younger fitter patients to needle and dialyse themselves.

This depressed mood is not continuous - it is more prominent during "dead" time, like Sunday afternoons, or some evenings. I try and avoid being passive like watching TV, but do other more active things, like attend the gym or walk in the park. I yearn to be with people to joke and have fun with them. Just the physical presence of others is a tonic and the boost to my mental health and feeling of well-being.

I struggle against the sense of loss that is happening all the time and the looming big loss as death approaches, and I will be no more. I have often thought about this by contrasting different forms of art - art that remains, like painting and sculpture, and art that disappears when it is over, like music, dancing or acting. My work is similar - when the meeting is over, it is over and it disappears, its benefits are in the changes to other people's lives, but my books can be read and re-read. Legacy has become more important since the start of dialysis. I am energised in book-writing and supporting the younger generation of psychotherapists, counsellors and consultants to write. As one of my early teachers frequently reminded us: "as much as the calf wishes to suck, so does the cow wish to suckle".

As I reflect on my journey with end-stage kidney disease and dialysis, I am acutely aware of the profound transformation it has brought to my life. From mastering the technicalities of dialysis to grappling with the emotional upheavals of a shifting identity, the experience has been both a physical and psychological odyssey. The transition from being a vibrant, active professional to someone reliant on a machine for life has been a challenging adjustment, fraught with moments of deep introspection and sadness. Yet, amid the loss and the looming presence of mortality, there remains a fierce determination to retain a sense of purpose and vitality. My efforts to engage with others, whether through writing, mentoring, or simply sharing a light-hearted conversation, are not just about maintaining normalcy but about asserting life in the face of an overwhelming sense of decline. This battle against the encroaching shadow of death is a testament to the resilience of the human spirit and a reminder of the enduring impact one can have, even as the sands of time slip away. In these final letters, I find solace and strength in the connections I forge, the knowledge I impart, and the legacy I leave behind. The journey may be arduous, but it is also a call to live fully, to love deeply, and to leave a mark on the lives of those around me.

Your loving father and grandfather, Mannie

Section 7

Letters to my Children

Letter #31

Thoughtful Concentration and Taking In

3rd March 2023

Dearest Shanan

After meeting you on Zoom on Sunday, I hope you do not mind me sharing some thoughts with you here.

The main thought I have is about how one "take things in" - something you described before in connection with your difficulties in concentrating. It seems to me that your concentration gets disturbed by the entry into your mind of other thoughts, like "what good is this thing you are doing or saying?", or "how am I going to remember what I'm learning?". Putting it another way, it seems that you do not trust the knowledge you are taking in to be available for you in the future when you may need it, as if you feel your mind is not capable of holding or keeping the knowledge in. This may be an expression of anxiety or/and depression that may have several sources. You sometimes give the impression of being surprised that someone knows something that you do not know or have not thought of before. Discovering that someone knows something that you do not know, and that you feel you should know, can be quite disconcerting and can lead you to reject what the other person is saying, just because the thought does not originate in you.

I felt that in your question at the end of our meeting of "what have I learned?" seems to suggest that you need reassurance that your memory is functioning and that you can recall what is in it. In fact, you remembered quite a bit of the material we covered, and you must have been quite satisfied, I reckon.

The conversation on Sunday then shifted to what happens to you on dates with women when you pre-judge the person and then proceed to confirm your pre-judgment which tends to prevent possible developments in the relationship. This may be connected to what I said in the previous paragraph about having and retaining knowledge, and grappling with the flip side of that, i.e. allowing enough space in your mind for new knowledge to enter and settle in. Relationships, among other things, concerns knowledge - knowing about your needs and simultaneously knowing and accepting the other person's needs; knowing when to step forward to meet their needs, and when to step back so that you don't create an unhealthy dependency.

I find it useful sometimes to think about my relationships with the universe. Sometimes I want to or need to control it; at other times, I tell myself I must wait for the universe to come to me, like waiting for signals to indicate what I should or should not do. Trying to control the universe (or other people) is exhausting, but it is also a sign of anxiety and depression that I do not know fully what is in me.

A few ways of developing skills in waiting for the universe to come to me include eliminating distractions, reducing multi-tasking, getting more sleep, taking short breaks, connecting with nature and training my brain to let things, including myself, just be, to stop striving.

Another term for not being able to concentrate well is brain fog. This may be caused by a nutrient deficiency, a sleep disorder, bacterial overgrowth from too much sugar, depression or a thyroid condition, chronic stress and a poor diet, or an untreated anxiety disorder, making relaxation impossible.

I am enjoying our Chevruta (joint learning sessions) very much and I hope you are too. As we get deeper into the material you may find it covers some of the things you talk about in your psychotherapy. Let us keep our focus on the study of dynamics at work, something that is sufficiently "out there", but also close enough to examine privately "in here, in me".

See you on Sunday,

Your loving father, Mannie

Letter #32

Educating our Children for the Spiritual Life

17th September 2022

Dear Shanan

I am choosing to write about this subject because I sense that your children may be struggling to get to grips with a satisfying spiritual side of life. I imagine this might be a difficult thing for them to do because of having lived through the difficult times of their parents' unyielding conflict with each other.

Spirituality can be said to be a search for meaning, a sense of wholeness, and leading a good, consistent life, free from the conflicting, puzzling and buzzing challenges that life throws at one. Parents, teachers and peers offer, and sometimes impose, restrictions on behaviour and depending on the manner of parenting, could leave the child with negative feelings about themselves to the extent that, through guilt and fear, they impose more extreme restrictions on themselves. This could affect the child's search for autonomy, agency, and identification with other people as role models. Our children are searching for their own autonomous identities, looking for a direction for their own unique ways in life that let them know who they are and where they are going, what choices they make that are best for them and for others with whom they share their lives. As a parent, one wishes to help our children avoid excessive confusion about the big moral questions of the day, to be able to differentiate between right and wrong, to be tolerant in relationships so that they can live their lives with less pain and conflict and achieve more satisfaction and joy.

Parents are obliged to provide safe, reliable, and loving environments so that very young children do not come to harm. At the same time, parents would want to limit the number of restrictions they impose on their children, so that they can develop a mature sense of themselves, can think for themselves and find good enough solutions, be flexible and adaptable, so that when the time comes, they can make and sustain loving relationships and continue their life's journey on their own terms. The ability to form good, affirming, and secure relationships is central. Our children need to feel comfortable with the range of their emotions, to know what they are thinking and feeling, and be able to share these in genuine, soft, pleasant physical and verbal communications that are expressed humbly and unpretentiously, without becoming frustrated, angry, or needing to dominate or control others.

Putting it another way, a parent would like to see their children be authentic about themselves and compassionate towards others, to express feelings thoughtfully and not be subject to shallow emotions; to be aware of the realities of the world and not adhere obsessively to only one point of view. As parents, we want them to be interested in others and in the wider issues of society and not have a narrow one-size-fits-all attitude. We want our children to be socially acceptable, not isolated and friendless, to be serious when seriousness is demanded, and to have a sense of humour and be fun-loving too, not dominated by guilt or anxiety, selfishness or aggression. We want them to be happy and relaxed, not stiff and formal, to be good citizens, and not filled with a sense of entitlement. We want them to be resilient and able to recover after disappointments, to get up and move forward again. We want them to be proud of their achievements and not conceited; to appreciate the achievements of others and not be envious; to applaud those who excel and support those who do not; to be creative themselves and enjoy the creativity of others; to be tolerant of their blind spots and not be critical of the blind spots and weaknesses of others.

Apologies if this sounds like a recipe for perfection; it is not meant to be – temperament, character, personality and life circumstances will influence the choices that our children make. These elements are not always under our control and, of course, we have our own unconscious dynamics to contend with - we, and they, should be satisfied with our children's choices and not get weighed down by unrealistic aspirations and regrets.

Your Loving Dad, Mannie

Letter 33

Collapse

26th May 2022

Dear Shanan, Yoram & Danny

I am writing to you about collapse - the sudden drastic breaking apart of political, economic and social complexity; the sudden loss of consciousness of the individual due to heat, seeing blood or shock, standing up quickly, dehydration or low blood pressure.

It is May 2022, and I am experiencing widespread collapse around and in me. A week ago, Mum collapsed in the kitchen as she bent down to get a vegetable out of a low drawer. She fell backwards, following what the ambulance crew called a head rush. She banged her head on the floor and fortunately she did not damage anything and after eight hours in A&E we returned home. Mum says she is anxious most of the time, has heart palpitations, which, of course, worries me too about imminent collapse. Her anxiety relates to my dialysis treatment for the collapse of my kidneys and the threat of losing me and having to live alone in her vulnerable state. She feels these events are echoes of Emily, her mother's final years of near total incapacity and being bedridden with 24-hour care. Added to her nightmare scenarios is the situation of your divorce, Shanan, after 27 years (that's another story) and the upcoming marriage of Hallel, and arranging the wedding with Sheera, your estranged wife, who appears not to want to collaborate to make Hallel's wedding day a happy occasion for her.

And Yoram's family all have got Covid, which they are getting over, thankfully.

And then there is the background social and economic collapse - the economy shuddering on the edge, cost of living spiralling wildly, and the war in Ukraine threatening to expand into World War III and with it the prospect of nuclear annihilation that could wipe out much of the world's population and civilization in catastrophic nuclear winters.

Everything seems so interconnected. The age we are living in as a family follows a lifetime of progressive improvement and development, and now it suddenly looks fragile and about to be extinguished. And this is happening in parallel in our society - the world folding in on itself after 80 years of reconstruction, progression, lifting whole populations out of poverty, dramatically increasing the number of people in the world, and raising standards of living.

Collapse - the return to dust, ruin and rubble - chaos. It seems we have believed all along in the wrong-headed idea that time, process, desire and ambition are linear in character in search of a glorious final objective, like the mythologies enshrined in our religions, as paradise, heaven - a place once achieved, we can relax into a state of infantile dependency and be sustained without further effort, a kind of ever-flowing stream of nourishment and fulfilment, devoid of further earthly toils. But perhaps the true course of nature (or life) is not linear, but circular, in repeated cycles of birth, growth, maturation, decline, decay and death - stages of life that we wrongheadedly cluster into benevolent or bad, or good or evil, and we leave it to the philosophers, religionists, moralists or politicians to sort out for us, so that we can shed the conflict and the mess from our minds and get on with our daily grind. And as we do so, we are shocked to see the sudden unfolding of monstrous evils that come to disturb our habitual taken-for-granted lives.

How do we prepare for and accept loss and death? It seems by denying them and choosing to believe in simpler linear equations and solutions to the complexities of existence that do not in fact lend themselves to linear thinking. We hear interminable sermons that living a righteous life leads to inheriting the world to come, or to politicians rallying cries for our votes so that they can get their hands on the levers of power and generate infinite improvements for us. For most of the population struggling to make ends meet, these dilemmas are largely left to the elites whom we revere and who personify the myths of invincibility but remain totally disconnected from themselves and from ordinary people.

As we navigate this complex and precarious time, the concept of collapse looms large, both on a personal and societal level. The recent events in our family—Mum's sudden fainting spell, the anxiety surrounding my health, the turmoil of Shanan's divorce, and the challenges of arranging Hallel's wedding amidst strained relationships—highlight how fragile our lives can be. This fragility mirrors the broader instability we observe in the world: the economic turmoil, the spectre of war, and the broader societal malaise. It seems that the linear narratives of progress and perpetual growth we have long embraced are unravelling, revealing a more cyclical reality. This reality is marked by periods of stability and growth followed by inevitable decline and chaos. In facing this, we must reconsider our perceptions of life's trajectory, acknowledging the impermanence and complexity inherent in existence. The challenge lies in preparing for and accepting loss and death, not as catastrophic ends but as integral parts of the life cycle. We must shed the comforting but deceptive notions of linear progress and invulnerability and instead embrace a more nuanced understanding that honours the cyclical nature of life. In doing so, we can find a deeper resilience and perhaps a measure of peace, even amidst the chaos and uncertainty that surrounds us.

Yours loving Dad, Mannie

Letter #34

Twin Grandchildren

5th January 2022

Dear Yoram

I have three sets of grandchildren, the latest set are your twins of three years old, Lily and Shiloh. Lily is the sweetest thing imaginable, engaging, loving, talkative and eager to learn. She is cooperative, tidy, wants to please and pays the biggest compliments to people. At times, she can be stubborn and self-willed, her span of attention is short as she seems to want to have so many different experiences at once. She is shy and fearful of strangers, and sometimes she shows that she does not want to be apart from you for any length of time. She has a small build and falls easily, but not seriously. Her twin brother, Shiloh, is a delightful child, fiercely curious about everything mechanical, is also engaging, asking a multitude of questions, wanting to enter every cupboard and empty its contents, unconcerned at the mess he is making. He runs around a lot, sometimes bumping into his sister, who has learned to hide under the table when he gets into his running phase. Each twin spends time separately in our house, but sometimes when they are here together, they form a gang against Leonie and me, speak a private language and create mayhem with the toys and other kitchen implements they manage to find. They both run around the table chasing each other to everyone's distraction. Sometimes, in their highchairs they will eat quietly, and suddenly on a signal, will throw food and plates around the room. For their elderly grandparents, baby-sitting can sometimes be exhausting, from walking after them, making sure they do not get into any danger to each other and to themselves, playing with them, organising them into separate rooms, changing them, dressing them if they want to go outside. But it must be said, baby-sitting can be hugely pleasurable, with quite deep and personal conversations with Shiloh and Lily. They like coming to our house and the opportunities it offers them to have fewer restrictions, as is usually the case with grandparents.

The complexity of family relationships and the dynamics of caring for grandchildren can bring both joy and challenges. The twins, Lily and Shiloh, each with their distinct personalities, enrich our lives with their energy and innocence. While Lily's sweet and cooperative nature brings ease, Shiloh's curiosity and liveliness present unique challenges that are just as precious. There is a delicate balance we all strive to maintain in showing equal love and attention to each grandchild. It is natural to feel moments of guilt or concern. However, it is essential to remember that these instances offer opportunities for reflection and growth. We affirm our love for both children, recognizing and celebrating their individuality which is necessary in the case of twins. Our role as grandparents is to support both twins in navigating their growth, offering them a safe space filled with love and understanding. The pleasure of witnessing their development far outweighs any momentary fatigue. Moving forward, Leonie and I aim to focus on nurturing open communication with Lily and Shiloh, ensuring that they feel supported and understood in their developmental journey. This should help foster a positive environment where both Lily and Shiloh can thrive.

Your loving Dad, and Grandfather, Mannie

Letter #35

Second Child

6th January 2024

Dear Yoram

Having young children keeps you young and fit, especially having a pair of delightful, but very active twins, who just love ganging up against others.

You have had an eventful life. Your early years were disrupted by our move from South Africa to London at the age of 1. At that age a child needs consistency and continuity as it is developing quickly and taking in many things that are going on around it, especially family tensions and anxieties. Mum and I were extremely distracted by simply trying to get by and survive in our new surroundings, in the UK away from our South African family networks, and inevitably probably we neglected your emotional needs. In your adult life, you trained in a very specialised form of physical fitness, after which you opened your own health-care business which you have managed extremely successfully for over 20 years. Your many clients who remain working with you for long periods, attests, not only to your competence, concern and commitment in the work you do, but also the affection, esteem and confidence that your clients have in you. You have the determination to succeed, you are resourceful and clear-thinking. You have adapted well to the strains of fatherhood which you entered later in life. Your delightful, clever children bring you and Lisa hours of joy (and some frustrations too), but the two of you have managed those very well indeed. Lisa's artistic side and her training as a nursery nurse show in the excellent mothering she provides and the artwork that Lily and

Shiloh produce and exclaim proudly when they rush into our house to show off their latest pictures and other lovely creations.

Although raising twins can be hard work, you also have the opportunity of observing their developing relationships, sometimes competitive, but mostly loving, caring and cooperative, first one is the leader and then the other, and their comradely followership, is also a lesson to behold. I'm sure there are many other lessons and joys to be had in observing their play and interactions.

I must add a word about our private moments in the gym, apart from the benefits the exercises give me, I hugely enjoy our conversations which cover everything from politics to military strategy, and from psychology to leadership. You have a broad general knowledge, you read widely, and you have well-developed views on the variety of important subjects. I'm often in awe of your intelligent espousal of your views around the dinner or lunch table. Putting it another way, you are admirably self-taught, you put historical facts and processes into perspective, and you speak on the radio in ways that attract attention. Well done, Yoram!

You are aware of the changing circumstances of Mum's and my life, and you have readily come to our assistance when needed. By being the only sibling near us, this must make you feel quite a burden of responsibility has been placed on you - we are very grateful for your help. You have participated in training to use the dialyzing machine and troubleshooting to help Mum should anything go wrong. We hope not to call on you in this regard, but it is comforting to know you are there and able to help should the need arise.

I must bring up what I suspect is probably on your mind, because it is on Mum's and my mind, and that is that we are both in our 80s, in not particularly good health, and the death of one or both of us is probably not far off. However much we want to ignore the subject of death, the fact is our weakening bodies are daily reminders of that inevitable eventuality. You should not be dismayed by this - Mum and I have come to terms with death being part of life - it comes to everyone including us. We only hope for a peaceful death that causes the least pain for everyone. Be strong and be aware that life, values, and memory carry on through our children and grandchildren all of whom we hold dear in our hearts. We hope you believe that despite the mistakes we made in your upbringing, we tried our best, with the limited knowledge we had at the time. But our love for you and our pride in you is deep and lasting. Let that be a source of strength for you - we had fun, and we laughed a lot at the absurdities of life. Let those be good memories for you. Following our passing, you will grieve, and the grieving will pass too, and you will revive and get on with your life. You are resilient, young and you have a strong constitution. You have tolerated and overcome many personal setbacks, you know the meaning of disappointment and you have survived many of them. I'm proud of you, Yoram, and I hope you can forgive me for my failures in your upbringing and in our relationship. I have thought about these often and wished I could have acted differently with greater kindness and understanding towards you. I've often thought of our commonalities - that we are both second children - and that we share the emotional psychology of being second children, struggling against the feeling of being inferior to or trying to keep up with an older, stronger, quicker and more able sibling. This second child status must have played a part in our relationship and perhaps not always beneficially because sometimes parents with unresolved conflicts from their childhood project their problems into the next generation, specifically into the second child, in the doomed hope that this child will in some way help to resolve the parent's unresolved emotional conflicts that come from being a second child.

This may sound complicated, but it is common in all parent-child relationships. To the extent that projections happen, I wish you to be free of mine, so I take back my projection of the second child syndrome into you and I hope this enables you to feel free to develop in your own independent way, without the burden of doing your father's emotional work.

In reflecting on your journey, Yoram, it's clear that you've faced numerous challenges with resilience and determination. Despite the complexities of raising twins later in life, you've managed to thrive personally and professionally. Your commitment to your family's well-being, coupled with the joy your children bring, is a testament to your strength and love. As your parents, we take pride in your accomplishments and cherish the meaningful conversations we share. Our love and pride are unwavering, and we hope you continue to find strength in these memories as you navigate life's ups and downs.

Your loving Dad, Mannie

Letter #36

Humour

1st May 2022

Dear Danny

Happy 50th Birthday, Danny!

Humour is felt when expected and rational behaviour occurs alongside statements or behaviour that is absurd or ridiculous; unexpected or surprising; or events that follow themselves in an odd sequence. The emotional experience of laughing and the sudden insights they produce make us aware of the absurdities of some life situations. Danny, you have a natural flair in playing with words with similar or double meanings and you are quick at putting them together in unusual and surprising connections. Seeing events evoking moral judgements addresses the depressive aspects of one's personality, judging people, events or statements in terms of good and bad, right or wrong. This level of seriousness can interfere with human relationships. Moral judgements originate in the part of the personality associated with guilt and shame. We defend ourselves against shame. Witness the struggle of the toddler mastering standing up and taking its first steps and often failing. 'Falling over' is commonly associated with clowning which parallels the young child's first attempts to stand and walk. The child may not get hurt, but certainly its pride is hurt, especially when to its parents who are watching the child's attempts to master uprightness and walking, can appear funny making them laugh and aggravating child's sense of shame. I recall many occasions getting things wrong and being laughed at, deepening my sense of humiliation, my face turning red, getting angry with the people laughing at me, and forgoing any more attempts to master that activity again, until I manage to master it perfectly. This may account for the drive towards perfection, fearing getting it wrong and being ridiculed. Schadenfreude is important here - taking pleasure or satisfaction in someone else's misfortune. For example, imagine a scenario where two competitive basketball teams have a long-standing rivalry. One team's fans, who have faced losses against the rival team many times, feel a sense of satisfaction when the rival team unexpectedly loses a crucial game against a third team. The fans' pleasure stems not from their own team's success but from seeing the rival team fail. Being the expert is a way of avoiding the shame of 'not knowing'. Curiously, an important element in developing psychotherapists and organisational consultants involves being able to tolerate 'not knowing', to regard the absurd as a central part of living, making mistakes, learning from experience, reaching into deeper recesses of emotion and learning to accept one's ignorance, failures and humiliations. The pursuit of solutions involves many twists and turns, and there is much to learn from curiosity, adventures and experiments. Humour involves timing – a good comedian is skilled in the mini-pauses when telling a good humorous story.

Once I was invited to propose a toast to our good friends on their wedding anniversary. I wanted it to be funny and produce gales of laughter. I found a funny story, rehearsed it well, improved my ability to control the pauses, and it went down very well with the audience who fell about the isles with laughter. At first, the flow did not come naturally to me, and I had to rehearse the story in front of a mirror several times - perhaps that is the lesson – humour sometimes stems from sizing up a situation naturally and re-presenting it in humorous form. In other cases, it takes significant rehearsal and practise to get it right. Humour makes the situation lighter; it can defuse anger or conflict by helping the parties see how ridiculous their fixed positions are. Comedians are often said to be sad inside, so perhaps humour and clowning are attempts to deal with their sadness when they are alone without an audience and only with themselves. Humour may be a defence against the tragedies of life, losses, and frustrations. The 'joker' in the group may be used by other group members to deflect away from difficulties in the group and may be used to prevent work from being completed.

Should the therapist/consultant laugh when something funny happens in the conversation? This dilemma is often debated in our work, and I wonder what would be so wrong about appreciating a humorous or funny situation. I would love to have your thoughts on this.

In conclusion, humour plays a multifaceted role in our lives, offering both a defence against the harsh realities of life and a means to lighten burdensome situations. Danny, your natural talent for wordplay and quick wit highlights the power of humour to create connections and offer new perspectives. While it can sometimes serve as a shield against shame and vulnerability, it also fosters understanding and empathy. Embracing the absurdity of life, even in professional settings, allows us to navigate complexities with grace and resilience. Happy Birthday!

Your loving Dad, Mannie

Letter #37

Restoration, Despair and Optimism

6th June 2022

Dear Shanan, Yoram & Danny

Alongside 'collapse', 'Restoration' must be considered important as an act of returning something to its former condition. The act is preceded by the desire to restore, to return to a previous state of being that is better than the present state. In my case, this desire is mostly frustrated by my age and state of health, but the desire is still there. I sometimes wonder whether it is nostalgia for an earlier idealised age or is it a fear of collapsing into a state of apathy, of stillness, of ceasing to be. My desire for restoration is strong. I still want to sort things out, attend to projects until they end at the agreed time, start new projects even though I may have to hand them over to someone else before I can complete them myself. I have put a lot of work into writing books with David, spending hours reordering the chapters into a different, more rational sequence, preparing my seminars and engaging with the middle-aged students who are 30 to 40 years my junior which is an age difference that I feel envious about. But I feel I am on their side, joining with them as they struggle to absorb new concepts and grow as a result. I'm looking for new projects and when I am busy on one, I feel a sense of rejuvenation, or fulfilment, almost like the frisson of a first date.

Restoration - returning something to its former condition - is a hugely positive life force when it happens, like building a model aeroplane, the repair of fractured relationships, the removal of painful feelings, especially feelings of abandonment and exclusion. We are sometimes encouraged to let go of past problems and move on, but that may be impossible if the thing you are trying to restore is important and is still fixable.

The restoration drive compensates for the destructive drives in ourselves and the resultant feelings of guilt that comes about through any perceived damage caused to people dear to us by our anger or rejection of them. We wish to restore them so that they and I can relate lovingly again, appear good and better than we were before, and we feel whole again inside. Couples often tell you their best sex happens after an argument. That is one example of the drive to repair; another might be the professions we choose, for example, medicine, nursing, social work and teaching, in which the drive to repair is strongly in evidence as a life choice over the long term. The wrong-headed aspects of these choices may emerge later when the career we have chosen is an externalisation of the restoration drive, i.e. repairing others and not consciously attending to the restoration of oneself and of early important figures, like parents. Externalisation of the restoration drive may mask the inherent destructive nature of the person, for example, the helping professional who compassionately cares for their charges, and who is nasty and sadistic to their partners and children.

This idea points to the striking duality of human experience - cycles of collapse and restoration. This is the reason why hope is so important - not only that bad external situations/things will change and be restored, but we also live in the hope that our inner world of feelings and emotions will change into wholesome loving and caring feelings which will be reciprocated by being loved and cared for in turn.

Despair

Despair is a common emotion too. How does one write when one is in the depths of despair, having no feelings, no thoughts, desire or energy - just an overpowering listlessness and lethargy? Wanting nothing, not wanting to do anything. Just wishing to remove oneself from the scene, a sense of bleak emptiness, a speck in the passage of time, with no markers, no place to rest, flying on until one runs out of fuel, drops into the sea and sinks helplessly beneath the waves. I wonder whether this dread occurs now because today is the day after my dialysis session. I am tired and drawn out after lying prone for 4 hours while my blood leaves me and is returned, only between 50% - 60% cleansed? Or is it because I sense the world, as I've known it, is disintegrating which in turn mirrors my internal disintegration, the difficulty of making connections, fulfilling obligations, and my traditional supports are no longer working as they once did? Dislocation is widely evident. Systems, like the NHS, airline travel, supply chains, energy supplies and local supermarket food stocks, are breaking down. Destruction features everywhere and in everything - in me, in Mum, in my children. I cannot escape how difficult it is to maintain optimism, relationships, integrity and a forward-looking attitude. Loss of control is an abiding experience, sinking beneath a morass of depleting demand - I have few resources left to replenish my tanks. The balance between my internal resources and external resources that I rely on are shifting - the coffers are emptying. It seems there is not enough to go round for everybody - rationing will have to come in.

Optimism

A good week has just ended, and I am feeling optimistic. Mum's dizzy spells are being treated by a skilled physiotherapist and she's feeling better with more treatments to come; Yoram is improving and getting back to work which strengthens him, and I have been taking up my professional roles in a reasonable manner. I am called upon to assist in a difficult situation over a complaint against the Institute and I feel I acquitted myself reasonably well, seeking to identify the predominant systemic dynamic that is influencing people's feelings, statements and behaviour. I am helped by my colleagues, and I feel I add gravitas that raises the level of conversation to a higher level, away from blaming and victimising individuals.

It's a strange thing this balance between optimism and despair - two sides of the same coin of being human and being born with and living with contrasting and contradictory sets of feelings and emotions - which set of feelings will predominate at any given moment? We seem to inhabit a world in which perpetual jollity and happiness is a 'must' and which denies the periodic existence of despair. Even where despair is permanent, it is possible to lift it through sympathetic interactions with other people. We need other people to gain perspective, to be reinforced; we need engagement with others listening, talking and emoting because it raises our levels of neurological health through the release of endorphins that enter our blood stream and produce feelings of well-being, feeling recognised and accepted and regarded as worthwhile.

How do I contend with an unexpected downturn in my life and the lives around me? During this past three weeks I have felt my world turn upside down. Instead of my days starting as they always have with a certain anticipation for the day's events ahead - the excited involvement with clients and patients in meetings and seminars, the joy of getting things done - during the past three weeks several health crises in members of my family and in me have produced a dread and fear of terrible things about to happen. The worst crisis happened to Yoram, falling victim to a hypertrophic obstructive cardiomyopathy, which necessitated an emergency ambulance admission to hospital where he spent five days, and had a heart monitor inserted into his chest. To cap it all, in hospital he contracted SARS, an infectious virus that potentially threatens Yoram's family. Next up, and this is where the wrong-headed idea seems to have made its appearance - after five days of immobility on a hospital bed, Yoram, on his return home, decided the lawn needed mowing, the garden needed weeding and newly delivered flat pack garden furniture needed constructing. His weakened back gave in and Yoram collapsed into a howling, screaming state in endless excruciating pain from which there was no relief. And being the weekend, no matter where we turned, no help was available from either the NHS or privately. The agony, and our helplessness, was unbearable. We could not find remedies anywhere; we watched Yoram descend into a terrible state of screaming, weeping and rage.

Eventually a doctor was found who administered an injection and prescribed painkillers, leading to an easing of Yoram's pain. Eventually Yoram was able to go back to his family. A second, stronger injection was administered yesterday; the condition, a ruptured disc, is expected to heal, and we are hoping this episode is over and that Yoram will accept that as a 56-year-old man with a heart condition, he will not be able to perform the heroic acts of a younger man, that he will be more cautious and tolerant of what he can and cannot do.

The next affliction is Leonie's dizziness that three weeks ago led to a fall, fortunately with no damage done, but leaving a residual dizziness that made her feel extremely vulnerable and anxious. Visits to a vestibular physiotherapist which was positive, involving a realignment of crystals in the inner ear, with only minor, short periods of dizziness. We wonder if the dizziness is the result of the cocktail of medicines she takes every day for her diabetes, heart palpitations and low blood platelets.

And then there is me on kidney dialysis three times a week with its implications - taking up six hours each time, including travel time, and the setting up of the dialysis machine, followed by the after-effects of headache, weakness and extreme tiredness, and a wasting of my body - muscle wastage, pallid, scaly skin, disturbed sleep pattern and a general slowing down of walking, speaking, eating,... i.e. living!

Then in contrast to this gloom, most days we babysit the twins, two of the most delightful, lovely children imaginable - engaging, curious, talkative and loving, but also the most active, agitated gang of two one could find - up to mischief, exploring everywhere, jumping and running in circles around the hapless adults who are meant to be looking after them. Stresses and strains from the descent into illness by so many members of my family at the same time are beginning to tell - nerves frayed, tempers are short, desperation is in the air, clear thinking is increasingly impossible; Mum and I live with a sense of imminent implosion in our lives and unlike our previous selves, we feel helpless to prevent it. Our family life appears to mirror what is happening widely around us in our society - a breakdown in the important systems we rely on - the near total absence of healthcare facilities, strikes in the transport systems that prevent me from reaching hospital for the dialysis on which my life depends, disruption at airports threatening to interrupt our family's travel plans, the rising cost of energy that upends our budgetary assumptions for the year, the reversion to coal-fired power stations because of the energy crisis, the churn in British government that increases the chaos at all levels of governance of the country, and a final apocalyptic threat by Mr Putin to destroy London with an atom bomb.

The planet too seems to be acting chaotically with massive changes in climatic conditions of extreme heat, cold and floods. Is the apocalypse upon us? Are we witnessing the collapse of society into an orgy of destruction once again? What has happened to the dream of a better future, a better society, of "they shall all sit under their own vines and under their own fig trees, and no one shall make them afraid...."? (Micah 4:4). Even getting Ukrainian wheat to a hungry continent is no longer possible because of wrong-headed thinking that Russia should in the 21st Century reclaim all the lands once conquered by Peter the Great - now its Putin the Great, wrong-headedly pursuing a fantasy of empire when the nations of the world are moving in the direction of independence of small parts and freedom to realign with new alliances. In the commercial world, laws exist to prevent or break up monopolies because they do not serve the public interest; yet Russia moves to create a huge monopoly in Eastern Europe with attendant dictatorships, repression and persecution of nations. How are we to understand these two competing forces in a world of growth and development, innovation and creativity: and the move towards compliance, militaristic discipline and loss of freedom and individuality?

How come the splits in the world's '-isms' based on valuing either the individual or devotion to the state are so extremely located in competing political systems of capitalism and communism? The Tavistock Institute of Human Relations for over a hundred years has stood up for the harmonious relating between the individual and group as a better safeguard against selfishness, narcissism and deadly ideologies. Hope of finding alternatives to humanity's tendencies towards splitting, cruelties and sadism, lie in constantly scrutinising ourselves, finding meaning in our lives that leaves room for different cultural, religious and political beliefs and systems. Rivalry, jealousy, envy and competition have their place in human affairs, but surely mechanisms can be established to limit their excesses. We expect individuals to exercise self-control. Could that not also happen in international relations? What fundamentally changes when individuals join together in groups? We get either football matches that provide for the acceptable expression of competition and aggression or Deep State that provides for psychopathic expressions of disregard of human values in the cause of the survival of the State, which really is just another human construct, and subject to similar and regular systemic cycles of growth, development, decline and death.

In this reflection, I explore the contrasting emotions of restoration, despair, and optimism. I have reflected on the desire to restore things to their former state, despite health challenges and aging, and the deep sense of purpose this brings. However, despair surfaces amid personal and societal disintegration, highlighted by my family's health crises. Yet, moments of optimism arise from professional achievements and family joys, balancing the bleakness. I have discussed the broader societal and global challenges, contemplating the duality of human experience and the potential for harmony and I have emphasized the importance of self-scrutiny and finding meaning amidst chaos, advocating for a balance between individual and collective well-being in a fractured world.

Your loving Dad, Mannie

Letter #38

Family Visits – Judaism & Psychoanalysis

3rd January 2023

Dear Shanan, Yoram, Danny and Children

Our London families have just had a momentous 3 weeks.

Our recently married granddaughter, Hallel and her husband, Eyal, came for two weeks; Shanan, our eldest son, and Hallel's father, flew over for five days, and Danny, our youngest son, and his two oldest children, Matar and Kerem, flew in for four days. Their time with us was lively and enjoyable through the frequent visits of our middle son, Yoram and Lisa, his wife, and their twins, Lily and Shiloh. It was a full house.

And then as quickly as they had come, they all went home and our house was empty again, filling Leonie and me with feelings of sadness, loneliness and an increasing sense of our ageing, our weakening bodies and minds, suddenly feeling listless, lethargic, unable to plan or decide on the smallest things. Even clearing up and doing the washing was a chore too far. And the big drama that happened on the day before Danny and his children were due to leave - Leonie, while reaching into a cupboard for a tin of beans had a blackout and crashed to the floor, banging her head against the wall as she went down and cutting her arm on the door post. I was upstairs when I heard a sharp thud and I knew immediately someone (Leonie or one of the twins) had fallen; I dashed downstairs to find Leone sitting on the floor, held up by a hugely distressed Danny, and Yoram applying his paramedic first aid skills to

Leonie's arm, and a few moments later, George, Leonie's huge Greek hairdresser, applying an ice pack to the rising bump on Leonie's head. Once the crisis was over and Leonie was bandaged up, we recalled that her fall was a replica of her collapse nine months previously on the day before Danny's departure for home.

Ageing and natural frailty apart, what, we wondered, was the possible connection between Leonie's fall and the anticipated sense of loss through Danny's, Matar's and Kerem's departure? How unconscionable are our separation feelings about our children leaving and the associated feelings of our own impending deaths? How the unspoken thoughts in everyone's mind consists of: is this the last time we will be seeing each other? The end of existence? Death at the doorstep, enacted now as a mini-death, as Leonie lay motionless on the floor? What unfinished business was still lying about which we should face while we still had the chance? Indeed, during the visits of the children and grandchildren, there were deep meaningful discussions with everyone, recalling our individual and family histories, including the traumas and the crises, old and recent, opening up old wounds and re-examining the pain. Around the Shabbat table on Friday night, the subject of my running away from my foster family at the age of 12 was brought up. This had a shocking effect on Matar (10), who pulled up a chair next to me and proceeded to ask me the most penetrating questions of what, why, when and then Matar, my young psychoanalyst-to-be grandchild offered me and others around the table a disarmingly accurate and compassionate interpretation of the dynamics that led me to be placed with my foster family and then to flee from it. Early next morning, while the adults sat around the breakfast table, we overheard Matar earnestly telling her brother Kerem (8) in the lounge, word for word, in Hebrew, the events of the night before. Both then presented themselves before me, and asked: "are you alright?"

Perhaps I should not have been surprised at the impact my story had on my grandchildren, but I was surprised at the impact they had on me - the conversations made me reconsider the effects of that early separation from my parents. During the following week, I discussed with my psychotherapist for the umpteenth time the possible effects of that early separation that I think I had suppressed for many years. Despite my deep professional involvement with the well springs of feelings and emotions and their influence on my patients' lives, the fact remains that I am probably emotionally quite shallow, fragile and cut off, and angry. My psychotherapist was reassuringly positive and pointed to my resilience and fighting spirit that sustained me and stayed with me during my struggles, even when answers elude me. To be sure, he also added that my work as a psychotherapist and consultant may serve my defensive needs too - working at my problems through working on the psychological problems of others, especially my patients and clients who were bringing to me their own anxieties about imminent endings and death.

Synagogue (Shul)

During the family visits, Shanan went to shul for the Shabbat service, and he came home full of praise for the joyful experience at the local Chassidic shul he had attended. He urged me to go (I had stopped going to shul since COVID three years ago). The people there, he said, were friendly and gave him a warm welcome. He had met some of his old school friends and they were overjoyed to see him again. So, I went to shul on shabbat which was also the second day of the festival of Shavuot (Weeks) and I was pleased I went. The community is small. I counted between 70 and 80 men and boys and about 40 women. The rabbi addressed the congregation and what he said made me think why I felt more at home at this Synagogue (from the Federation of Synagogues) then I do at the large cathedral synagogue of Kinloss Gardens (of the United Synagogue establishment), which is down the road in the opposite direction. The rabbi in his sermon referred to the waves of immigration at the turn of the 20th century from Eastern Europe of people who did not quite fit into the culture of the establishment United Synagogue, so they established their own system of shuls that today number about 30 to 40 communities, mostly in London, but also a few in the provinces. The communities of the Federation of Synagogues are small, compact, religiously quite orthodox, but sufficiently modern and inclusive so that even non-practising Jews can find a place in them.

During the service, a thought of the prodigal son went through my mind. I am quite familiar with the order of the prayers, the melodies (and boy! Do they belt them out) and the wonderful post-service kiddush chatting and eating. I can easily find my way around and I even know how to lead certain services. But I had become a stranger in my own 'home'. Was this, I wondered, an extension of the foreign-ness, an "un-belonging", that resulted from having prematurely lost the home into which I was born?

This led me to another thought - just as the Federation of Synagogues became the home of foreign Jews who could not assimilate into the establishment United Synagogues, I wonder whether the Tavistock Institute of Human Relations and the Tavistock Clinic, where I have worked in different roles for the past 50 years, had been the home to many who had fled authoritarian regimes, or had had difficult and disrupted childhoods themselves – *abandoned orphans,* like Moses, as Dr Eliat Aram, CEO, had once spoken about? "The Tavistock" is an institution with which people can identify, both as a safe haven and also with its culture of deep scholarship and practice that is devoted to the pursuit of discovering different ways of living and relating. It is an institution where the collective experience of researching "strangeness" is put to good use by social scientists of many disciplines who explore the mysteries and 'strangeness' of human behaviour across a broad spectrum of social functioning, good and bad.

This led me to recalling my experiences as director and consultant at the Tavistock Institute's well-known Leicester conferences and as an organisational consultant in project work. Consultancy, as practiced at the Tavistock Institute is a role that "sits on the boundary". One works with the group, but with a different role to the rest of the group - one 'sits on the boundary' between what is inside and what is outside; not so close and involved as to be caught up in the group's dynamics, and therefore, less able to be of use to the group in the business of learning; and not so far removed from the group, as to be disengaged from the task of learning. This leads me to think that people who have "on-the-boundary personalities" are more likely to do better in therapeutic and consultancy work because they have a role which requires skills to observe what is happening in the group while retaining the freedom of thought to help the group move on in its chosen journey.

Extrapolating this idea to Jews and Judaism, I come up with something similar. The origin of Jews and Judaism lies in its challenge to existing beliefs, practices, values, morals and social structures. The root of the word "Hebrew" (Ivri) is "from across" or "to bring across". The Hebrews came across the Jordan river - also a metaphor for standing across from prevailing understandings of the cosmos and understanding of life on this earth. Assumptions underpinning local beliefs about creation, the meaning of existence, were, and continue to be, openly challenged, and like psychoanalysis of the present day, these challenges are generally resisted, because no matter how wrong-headed a belief may be, they are often held onto uncritically and desparately as if they are matters of life and death.

Therefore, it is important to make a distinction between the credo and the people practising that credo, because strong convictions tend to turn credos into unthinking dogmas of the masses and empty rituals, based on hysteria, anxiety and guilt which are often performed unthinkingly.

These musings lead me to believe that I am what I am, and I must accept that I am a 'boundary person' with a foot in both camps - Judaism and psychoanalysis - and I embrace them both critically and in the fullness of joy and creative discovery, taking up my Jewish identity where appropriate, and my psychoanalytic identity where appropriate. I accept that both systems of thought can exist side by side, with both enjoying my respect and awe for what it purports to offer humankind, and acknowledging their limitations, which is then complemented by other bodies of knowledge that offer additional understandings of the human condition in all its aspects. And where there are conflicts between the demands of these two identities, I will attempt to do my best and judge for myself which demands to follow.

In this reflection, I recount a recent family gathering, filled with lively moments and meaningful conversations, highlighting the joy of connection and the inevitability of separation. The departure of my family leaves me and Leonie feeling lonely and confronted with our mortality, especially after Leonie's fall, which evokes fears of loss and the finality of death. The experience prompts me to introspect on unfinished family business and the impact of past traumas.

I also reflect on my Jewish identity and experiences at the synagogue, finding a sense of belonging yet feeling like an outsider. I draw parallels between my roles in psychoanalysis and Judaism, both of which challenge established norms and offer deep insights into the human condition. Ultimately, I embrace my dual identity, acknowledging the coexistence of both perspectives and their contributions to understanding life. I accept the complexities and conflicts of my roles, resolving to navigate them with respect, joy, and critical inquiry.

Your loving and sceptical father and grandfather, Mannie

Letter #39

Various – Writing, Psychoanalysis & Dream

3rd February 2023

Dear Children and Grandchildren

I am sitting in my office facing an empty white page on which I hope to write a tale that addresses an important life issue. I suppose, like a lot of people, my mind turns to the crisis the world is in and wonder how we got here. I recall childhood conversations with my cousin, Lenny, in Port Elizabeth after the Second World War, age 5 or 6, discussing very seriously what life we were going to lead - an American way of life or a Russian way. I think we opted for an American way because we saw flashy American cars around us, we watched American films and saw American style advertisements around the place. We understood that America was strong and wealthy.

4th February 2023

Hello journal! I have accumulated so many thoughts and stories, I don't know where to begin. Perhaps with a dream - a worrying one. Leonie and I are walking somewhere in South London, unfamiliar territory, and I don't know what bus to take to get back home. I hesitate; we are not even standing at a bus stop. Leonie gets impatient and without a word, she walks off, ignoring me and I hear her footsteps receding in the distance.

I'm not writing enough, not writing at all. I wonder what am I avoiding? I know that attending to underlying feelings, memories, etc., provides relief and a sense of accomplishment, doing something useful for me and for others. Why am I not writing, but instead letting practical arrangements fill most of my time? To be sure, getting my room ready for home dialysis requires time and effort and emotional energy, for it involves throwing out old papers, files and notes of my psychotherapy practice to donate to the Tavistock Institute archive.

The Tavistock archive is a wonderful institution and research facility, as I discovered when I used it for a talk on the work of Isabel Menzies Lyth and for our work on a new book on Eric J. Miller's life. This archive contains their work, arranged neatly in files, that opens a window on how they thought about their work, their clients and the social institutions and systems of their day. Nothing short of inspirational. And then I remember the conversation with Eliat in which she spoke about my files going into the archive for use by future researchers. I like the idea and it makes sorting the papers that much easier and purposeful, not to mention that part of me that is thinking about my legacy, about what I leave behind, allowing for the expression of my vain side and accepting that though I am not in the same league as Miller, Rice and Menzies Lyth, I have contributed to changing people's lives and to the development of new knowledge by putting things together in new ways. After all, how can new discoveries be made when the original ideas were discovered generations ago? How does one introduce a freshness into old ideas instead of regurgitating them endlessly until the life is taken out of them?

Some of this feeling of being an innovator comes from co-authoring three large volumes with my colleague, David Lawlor, called *Systems Psychodynamics* in which we make a strong case for the term to refer to a new paradigm. I'm proud of that and it is supported by the range of theories and their applications that are described in the trilogy. The feedback has been positive, and people have written gratefully to say our books have influenced their thinking and practice.

Another source of strength is the conversations I'm having with my psychotherapist, who is also an author of books and who writes beautifully and comprehensively about both the positive and negative sides of human nature, never forgetting that people are made up of many parts - some constructive and some aggressive and destructive.

And of course, there is Leonie, who has lots to be depressed about, and who nevertheless is a perennial optimist who encourages me to look on the bright side of things.

Press on, press on. You have 20 minutes before you must leave this page. "Write it down" is the title of a wonderful book on writing - something, anything from the unconscious where everything is stored. Oh yes! A memory of Emmanual Hall, 1947, where I attended first year of school, Standard I. My mother comes into the classroom to talk to the teacher, and because she is my mother, I feel I have the right to be different, to cut a little slack, to leave my seat and walk up to her to show I can be different because it is my mother who is here, but she will have none of it. She's embarrassed by me and 'shushes' me back to my seat. She does not condone the breaking of rules and shows that she is subservient to the authority of the teacher, as she was to the authority of doctors that led disastrously to the breakup of my family. What was she doing in the classroom? I don't know, but I imagine she came to tell the teacher something about me - perhaps to explain about my asthma and to ask the teacher not to let me run around because that brings my asthma on. I remember the teacher's name - Mrs Newman - I also remember where I sat and what I was doing - at a desk on the left of the classroom towards the back and we were doing writing, and I remember making the word "going" and feeling please with my mastery of the participle from "go" and "ing". I sometimes wonder if my interest in the written words may have started there? I cannot say I was a regular reader or pursued literature with any great enthusiasm, but I did read quite a lot, and I remember a description of the artistic form of the letter "a" and how all letters have their distinctive artistic quality. When I learned Hebrew, I was impressed by the literal meanings of letters and their relationships to the lives lived by people in the Iron Age. For example, the 2nd letter of the Hebrew alphabet is 'beth' and it looks like this in print form (ב). The Hebrew for house is 'bayit' and indeed the 2nd letter 'beth' is shaped like a house. And so, I could go on for the third letter, 'gimmal' (ג) and the word "Gamal" meaning "camel" and the letter looks like a camel. The letter "mem" (מ) resonates with the word "mayim" which means 'water' and the letter looks like a vessel for containing water. Signs and names in the biblical stories of houses, camels and water, are symbols representing real objects and form; these real objects moved to ideas, to cultural behaviours and to morals becoming the fabric of social interaction, social cohesion and these artefacts pass mysteriously from one culture to another.

I have written thousands of letters and yet I am not a man of letters. I strive to write well and communicate straightforwardly. I belong to the "People of the Book" and I respect the printed word. I have published books, but I'm not an author; I like writing, but I procrastinate and do not have the discipline of setting regular writing time. I encourage others to write but do little of it myself. From my analytic experience, I have discovered my competing selves and how they undermine each other and get in the way of getting things done, as if the prospect of accomplishing something worthwhile and praise-worthy is deliberately avoided - this is surely evidence of the envy I have towards parts of myself, and the fear of other people's envy towards me.

Reading Michael Brearley's stupendous book: "Turning Over the Pebbles", a memoir of his mind, as his editors suggested, is a book to his grandchildren, and it has been an inspiration in how to bring disparate paths of one's life together, to make sense of feelings and events of earlier times and to experience their meanings differently. Michael writes at length about the prospect of death and offers the reader hope that even death can be meaningful, despite a general impulse to avoid it. Do we use religion as a sop against the fear of not existing?

In this reflective journal entry, I grapple with unexpressed thoughts and emotions, symbolized by a troubling dream where Leonie walks away, leaving me lost and uncertain. I express frustration at not writing enough, despite recognizing the therapeutic benefits of confronting underlying feelings and memories. Preparing for home dialysis and sorting through decades of professional papers evoke thoughts about legacy and contributions to the Tavistock Institute archive, which might inspire future researchers.

I contemplate my life's work, including significant contributions to *systems psychodynamics* and the influence of my books. I acknowledge the encouragement from my psychotherapist and Leonie, who, despite her struggles, remains optimistic. A memory from childhood surfaces, illustrating early feelings of differentness and the beginnings of a fascination with written words. I reflect on my relationship with writing—admiring it but often procrastinating. I recognize a conflict within myself, where competing desires and fears undermine my efforts.

Inspired by Michael Brearley's memoir, I find hope in facing the inevitability of death, contemplating whether religion is a comfort against the fear of nonexistence. This reflection concludes with an acceptance of my multifaceted self and the ongoing journey to reconcile competing aspects of my identities.

Yours, etc., Mannie

Section 8
Letters to my Grandchildren

Letter #40

Athletics – Matar

17th August 2022

Dear Matar

At 10 years old, you have started doing athletics, and I understand you are a pretty good runner, so I thought I would write to you about running and the impact it had on me when I discovered at about the same age as you are now, that I could run quite fast. I was also surprised to discover that near the end of the races I ran, I could still find the energy to give the last 100-200 metres an extra burst of furious running, overtaking the exhausted runners in front of me, to become the winner or take the second or third position.

I spent more time on the track and enjoyed the experience of running, finding that I was developing a philosophy of running, and I thought I would share some of these thoughts with you. Perhaps you have discovered this for yourself - that when you run, your mind opens to thoughts that you would not necessarily have when you are not running. Books have been written about running and philosophy and I can recommend one to you: *Running and Philosophy: A Marathon for the Mind*, edited by Michael Austin (you can borrow mine, when you next come to London).

Running stimulates many questions: is running a way of dealing with angry feelings? Is running a sort of religion? After all, to be good at it, regular practice, done religiously, is needed, timing yourself to tenths of a second. Is running an attempt to unravel the nature of happiness? Others ask: does the pain one feels during running exertions have meaning, come to teach us something? How should we serve our communities? Running certainly is motivated by feelings of wanting to do well, as much for oneself as one's organisation or team. Is running an art like other artistic quests? Whether you think these questions, or others like them, running certainly provides time and space for thinking.

Other people sometimes say running is a strenuous physical activity, a strain on the heart and legs, but runners will tell you, that if you're fit, the heart and the legs go into automatic mode, and we become almost pure of mind as we run. Away from home, our desks, our friends, and meetings, we run automatically and there's nothing else to do but think - musicians compose, writers write, actors rehearse, philosophers work on the Big Question. We run therefore we think, and the results can be deep. Runners are often said to be waging a war with their internal demons, overcoming their physical weaknesses, agonising over whether to give up or fight on, conquering feelings of inferiority to become a hero, hoping to transform into an angel with winged feet.

In my adolescence, I was full of inner conflicts (you can almost see them in my photographs), many drives, mixed feelings, and unanswered questions about the universe. I was not interested in the fake consolations that others around me were giving me. I think at that point, I had vague thoughts that meaning and value must be constructed by me, and they would be fragile, although then I mostly thought the fragility existed in other people, not me. Running to beat my rivals or the clock helped me see the challenges of life more positively, to recognise that feelings of revenge or resentment were distractions, and to accept fate as it is, respecting the order of things based on merit, taking opportunities when they turned up, for improving my performance through struggle and love of life, and to give up useless ideas of being saved. I thought that if I confronted my life creatively (it's the only one I've got) and with a full heart, that would be quite enough.

Matar, you will run to improve your fitness levels, and to test your capabilities. You will attain your personal best performances and achieve your individual goals, regardless of where you are placed in the race. You will try and do your best against your own limitations and weaknesses, the forces of nature, like the weather, and you will be willing to accept calmly that the performances of others in the race may sometimes be superior to your own. All this takes discipline, hard work and not being afraid to take risks. The loneliness of the distance runner is like a mirror of the lonely struggles you will have to face to become a worthy person and to construct your individual identity. Training for athletics requires discipline, overcoming obstacles, refusing to give up, high energy and exertion and chasing after a worthy goal. You will battle against your own psyche, not give in to your doubts, but instead you will have the will to achieve power and extend your influence through your boldness, creativity and innovation. I believe in you!

Your questions are bound to be about the practical aspects of running, so here are a few tips and hints to help you run better and faster. Like other aspects of your life, running requires planning, practice, technique and a bit of luck.

Four weeks before a race: in the weeks before a race, you need to pay attention to exercise, diet and sleep.

Exercise: (i) once every day, you should do lumbering up and stretching exercises. Good exercises include raising your arms up as high as you can reach, while raising your legs to stand on tip toe, and deep breathing on the up movement and breathing out on the down movement. Repeat this exercise 10-15 times slowly.

(ii) raise your arms as high as they can go and bend down from the waist without bending your legs and touch your toes. Repeat 10-15 times.

(iii) Jumps. As you jump, clap your hands above your head and spread your feet out wide to the side, while breathing in. Jump back to the attention position – feet together and lower your hands to your sides while breathing out. Repeat 10-15 times.

(iv) Lie on your back, legs stretched out in from of you. Slowly pull your legs together up to your chest while breathing in and slowly let them return to the rest position on the floor while you breath out. Repeat 10-15 times.

(v) the same as above, but instead of bringing your feet up to your chest together, bring them up to your chest one at a time, then let the leg down to the ground and pull the other one up to your chest (like pedalling on a bicycle) – all the time breathing on the up movement and out on the down movement. Repeat 10 -15 times.

For four weeks before the race: go to the track or park and run about 2 or 3 times a week. Divide the distance you intend running into 4 parts – run the first part slowly; run the second part a little faster, the 3rd part slowly and the 4th part a little faster. (Notice by the end of the 2nd week of doing this, how much fitter you feel.)

Diet: eat wholesome foods – salads, vegetables, small amounts of fish, meat and chicken, only small amounts of starchy foods like potatoes and bread. Avoid fizzy drinks, sweets, ice creams and cake. Drink 1 to 2 litres of water a day.

Sleep: Try and get to sleep early and aim for 7 hours sleep a night.

Footwear and clothing: run in good well-fitting footwear and wear tight-fitting clothing, nothing that could obstruct your movement. When you practice, wear a track suit over your running gear; when you are racing remove your track suit moments before the race.

Toilet: go to the toilet about 1 to 2 hours before a race – you don't want to be carrying unnecessary weight!

Hair: Tie your hair back tightly.

Planning: Planning is important, but you should also be flexible about it. Sometimes you may have to change your training schedule, increase it or reduce it. Your planning should include visiting the layout of the track or other places where the race will be taking place. Visit and walk over the distance of the track. Figure out at which spot you will be following the first two or three runners, and at which spot you will be putting in your final burst to overtake them. If you will be running over open country, that is, not on an athletics track, notice where the land rises and where it descends and work out how much more energy will be needed to run uphill and how much breaking you will need to run downhill. Notice the signposts where you will have to turn left and right. You want to avoid making mistakes which could cost you valuable seconds.

If you can, you should run regularly on the track where the race will take place, getting used to timing yourself and shaving seconds off your time at each practice run.

Imagination: each time you run, and even when you are not running, it is a good technique to imagine yourself running – the start of the race, the middle part and the final part; imagining your feet flying each step in front of the previous step. Imagine yourself in relation to the other runners and see yourself in your mind overtaking them one at a time until you are in front of all the runners heading for the final tape.

Technique: you will develop your own techniques that suit you best, but one good technique is to keep just behind 2 or three of the front runners. These runners are usually called the pace setters for the person who is eventually going to win. In a manner of speaking, they "pull" the winner along by their fast pace, but they cannot keep it up until the end and they make way for the winner who comes up from behind. Preserve your energy for the final 100 to 200 meters and you race ahead, overtaking them and run furiously to win.

Technique also involves breathing properly and deeply. My technique was to breathe in on the left foot and breathe out on the next left foot.

Remember too, to run on the inside of the track, not the outside because the outside is a longer distance. Of course, you may have to run on the outside briefly when you overtake other runners but get back to the inside as quickly as you can without cutting in front and obstructing the runners you are overtaking.

Focus on yourself and your running movements, be aware of where the other runners are in relation to you, without looking back – that could cost you seconds. Do not pay any attention to the crowds watching.

Luck: sometimes you need luck in where you are placed at the start; you need luck regarding the weather, the wind, and the condition of the gravel on the ground. Avoid loose stones and gravel.

A good technique is do not tell the other runners what your technique is.

Confidence: having confidence to win goes a long way to helping you win. Dream of winning and think of winning, and you will win.

Your loving grandfather, Mannie

Letter #41

Not Losing (Athletics)

30th August 2022

Dear Matar

I heard that you did not win the race that you had hoped to win for your school. You must be disappointed because you worked hard during your training before the race. You wanted your team to win, and you hoped your contribution would help your team to do so. The photograph of you towards the end of the race shows the strain on your face as you struggle to keep up with what look like much older children. I also understand that you did not pace yourself well; that you ran very fast at the beginning and used up most of your energy that you needed for the end of the race. Perhaps you were anxious and felt you needed to be ahead of the pack from the beginning.

I'm writing to you about the experience of not winning, which is not the same as losing. In athletics we run to beat the other runners, or the clock, or sometimes both, runners and clock, at the same time. We also run to enjoy the exciting sensations of exerting our bodies to move through space speedily. There are many ways to enjoy running and I hope you had those too. By not winning, or not doing as well as you had hoped, may also cause you to feel disappointed, embarrassed, or even make you feel shame - perhaps for disappointing others, like your friends, family and teachers. Painful feelings like these can affect your running by undermining confidence in yourself and in your running abilities. That would be a pity. So, I am writing to describe the positive side of not winning. And this has to do with learning. It is said that we learn more from our mistakes than from our successes. When we are successful, we tell ourselves that to succeed in the next race, all we need do is repeat what we did before, but in order to succeed again, repeating what we did before is not the best formula; we need to learn to do better through introducing new techniques, new strategies, to experiment with new methods, seeing what works and what does not. But the key to learning from not winning, is to keep alive the spirit of trying, not to let yourself be overcome with feelings of failure, which can be devastating, we all know. You were faced with a difficult challenge - a 1,200-metre race is a long distance for a 10-year old; and running against older children makes it even more difficult because they have longer legs, larger lungs and more running experience. Learning from not winning involves resilience - that feeling of determination to try again and do better, of which you have plenty in your character and that shows up in other areas of your life.

You have a wonderful philosophy, Matar, which you express in your daily life in the modest and kind things you do for people. Like you said, you would share your running techniques with the rest of your team because you run as a team and not only as individuals. That is another kind of winning - the huge satisfactions that come from working together with others as a team, to participate in the race, play your part in the team that leads to others winning, everyone working collectively to help one person get over the line.

Your Loving Grandfather, Mannie

Letter #42
Desire – Adeena

28th February 2022

Dear Adeena

Following our discussions about what career path to follow, I want to share with you what drove me to express my desire about what I wanted to do with my life. It started like this – one day when I was 15, I attended an ice show matinee at the Johannesburg Ice Rink. Since the show was in the afternoon, there were many children with their parents there, but in addition there were groups of disabled children in wheelchairs, some walking with walking sticks, others being led by the hand, several nurses and other carers. I had never seen so many disabled people at the same time in one place before. The intensity of the experience was overwhelming. I recall watching these disabled children more than watching the show. And then at the end of the show, I watched fascinated, horrified and overcome with a terrible sadness as the groups of children were wheeled out or led out, to their special buses, children with Down's syndrome, children who had stiff limbs or other abnormal muscle tightness, forcing them into hideous walking disorders, pulling grotesque faces, dribbling, mumbling or shouting, or talking from a space deep inside themselves. It was the first time I heard the term cerebral palsy. I remember coming home from the show with my mother and sister, looking out the window of our comfortable home in Emmarentia at the beautiful sunset over Northcliff, a steep plateau about 5 miles away, and declaring stridently and in a choking voice, that I had made my mind up to become a paediatrician. The urge to care for these children, to do something to alleviate the crippled-ness of their limited, and to what seemed to me to be extremely unhappy lives, possessed me. My mother and sister looked at me surprised and a bit shocked that I was so moved, indignant, even angry. I thought they seemed relieved that I was no longer this undecided boy, who did not know what he wanted to do with his life, that he had found his mission. I think in the short-term, they were relieved that I was turning 'normal', about to follow the traditional Jewish and family journey into medicine, the hope of almost every Jewish mother. I think my mother was also relieved that perhaps now I would apply myself to my schoolwork to get the good grades I would need to get into medical school. I am not sure how long this desire to become a paediatrician lasted; I recall it lasted a long time and I did apply myself to my schoolwork, but other experiences and events came along, and I moved in a different direction, but never giving up my desire to offer 'service', to remedy situations that I felt were unjust and should simply not be. This included growing powerful feelings to 'remedy' the Jewish situation and I turned to Zionism, feeling the profoundest desire to contribute to establishing a secure state for the Jews in Israel, that would take in the 'cripples' and 'misfits' of the world and transform them into 'normal' people. I was overflowing with love of Zionism and desire to play my part in the re-establishment of a national entity for the Jews after 2,000 years of exile. I was just one generation away from the effects of this terrible Jewish story of exile – my father had emigrated from Lithuania in 1928 and lucky for him too, because those he left behind were murdered by the Nazis in December 1941. I have the documents that confirm this. My mother's parents too had emigrated from Lithuania at the turn of the Century, and they had produced nine children – 6 boys and 3 girls – and in good Jewish tradition, the girls married, and the boys became shopkeepers and businessmen. Several of the third generation, my mother's nephews, became doctors and professionals, and that was where I was headed, inspired by a maddening drive to 'fix' things, to remove injustice, ill health, inequality and poverty. I saw this in two contexts – the oppressed, rejected black people in a prosperous South Africa in which most Jews were in the ascendency, and Jews in the diaspora, a dispersed and despised people, helpless, hunted and murdered in their millions. I could not make sense of these dichotomies, and I hoped and prayed that I would be useful and instrumental in bringing about their salvation. It was a kind of life mission. I could not think of any other avenue in my life than taking a lead in changing world history through a universal re-orientation away from the iniquities of race hatred, prejudice and humiliation into a state of total acceptance as equals, a system of living based on equal opportunity for all on lands that offered bountiful resources and enough for everyone.

In my journey, I have realized that the path to achieving these goals is multifaceted. I have sought to understand the complexities of human suffering and inequality, which has led me to explore various fields such as law, social activism, and international relations. Each step has reinforced my commitment to making a difference, whether through direct service, advocacy, or policy-making. My experiences have taught me the importance of empathy, resilience, and the power of collective action.

Adeena, I hope my story inspires you as you navigate your own career path. Remember that the drive to make a difference can take many forms, and each experience will shape and refine your vision. Trust in your journey, stay committed to your values, and know that your passion to create a better world will guide you to where you are meant to be.

Your loving grandfather, Mannie

Letter #43

The Love of Sharing

20th September 2022

Dear Lily and Shiloh

Although you are still three years old, I am writing to you in the hope that when you read this, some years from now, my letter will have meaning for you and will let you know how much joy you brought into our lives. Grandma and I were nearing our 80s when you were born and I brought you and your dear parents from the hospital to live in our house, which you did a for a year before your family moved to a home of your own.

During the year you stayed with us, we shared with your parents some of the functions of parenthood, feeding you, changing you and also taking great pleasure in having babies in our house again. Grandma and I had had previous experience of having babies and young children around us, but never before did we have the experience of living with twins. You presented us with a wonderful opportunity of observing how twins develop and grow, in themselves and in relation to each other. It was amazing that there were always two of you, and we saw how comforting and reassuring it was for each of you to have the other. I vividly remember the first time when you were about 8 or 9 months old, you were lying in your mother's arms and you both looked into each other's eyes in an act of real physical recognition. A half-smile crossed your faces, as if you had found someone you recognised and whom you were happy to see. It was an incredible moment, like making a new discovery of someone who looked like a mirror image of yourself.

As time went by, your relationship with each other deepened, became more intense and loving. Whenever one of you received something special, you would ask "one for Shiloh?" or "one for Lily?". The two of you also found ways to get around the adults, speaking your own private language which no one else could understand. Your shared thoughts and behaviour gave you power to escape from the rules and restrictions imposed on you by the adults and you seemed to revel in it, which was wonderful to see, even though it was exhausting for us. You were lively, cute, utterly adorable and terrific to engage with, as conversations between us became more commonplace and addressed your numerous questions of "why?". Without a doubt, your imagination and ability to play out scenarios were impressive and engaging. I had hours of joy imagining with you our struggles to defeat animal monsters, climb high mountains, fly through the air, crawl through the jungle, swim in the ocean, build towers and break them down again, cook meals and feed everyone. When we tired of all that activity, we sat quietly and read books together, when we could once again let our imaginations wander and visit exciting places with wonderful animal friends.

Of course, there were times when you would argue over who got what, like who got the better toy, but there was something about "twinship" that was more about sharing than about competing. You comforted each other when you were frightened of strangers or squirrels or wolves or foxes. Those moments of comforting one another were a testament to the deep bond you shared, a bond that I hope will continue to strengthen and support you both throughout your lives.

Your presence in our home brought a new vitality and sense of purpose to our days. The laughter, the discoveries, the challenges – they all contributed to an unforgettable year that Grandma and I cherish deeply. Watching you grow and develop, seeing the world anew through your eyes, has been one of the greatest joys of our lives.

As you continue to grow, I hope you carry with you the love and lessons of your early years. Know that you are part of a family that values compassion, resilience, and the pursuit of justice. Your innate curiosity and sense of wonder are gifts that will serve you well in your journey. Embrace them, nurture them, and let them guide you to create a life filled with purpose and fulfilment.

Your loving and doting grandfather, Mannie

Letter #44

The Conflict between Self-interest and Loyalty to Others

Acknowledging the Success of Others and the Help they Give.

17th March 2022

Dear Adeena

This is an interesting question that will confront you from time to time in your life - when should I consider my interests over my responsibilities towards others, and when do my interests take second place in favour of other people's interests or needs? These challenges confront us more often than we realise. How we resolve them tells us something about our character and about how we will behave in the future.

Self-interest starts early in the first moments of life. A life force, called Eros, drives the infant; it must breathe, take in nourishment and eliminate and clear away its waste. These are survival instincts and, of course, the infant at first does not "think" about them consciously, because it does not yet think in the way that adults think about thinking. But as the infant turns into a toddler, we notice that it becomes quite self-centred, able to say, as it often does, "I want ..." or "I do not want ..." and it does not spare a thought over whether what it "wants" or "does not want" might inconvenience others, especially its mother. The toddler expects its mother, (and others) to be always available and willing to deal with its desires, needs and fears. Only later at about the age of three or four does the young child become consciously aware that its mother (and others, although at first, this will be a vague awareness) is a person in her own right, who is sometimes there and thinking about the child, and sometimes she is not there. She may be feeling miserable, attending to others, she may be feeling hurt, as the child itself sometimes feels miserable or hurt. This growing awareness in the child that its mother has feelings (and has relationships with others), helps the child to moderate its expectations, to feel compassion and consideration for its mother and begins to respect her autonomy - the beginning of responsible socialisation. The young child learns that it may have to wait, that its mother's responses do not always satisfy it, that an angry or desperate reaction to its mother's slowness or refusal to satisfy it at once, may not be the best way of getting what it wants. The child discovers that suspending its demands or responding to what its mother, or other siblings want, produces its own rewards, like receiving praise for considering others.

So, when in later life, when we have established our personalities, and we can balance our self-interest with attention to the needs of others, sometimes something will occur to disturb that balance, and we may have to re-evaluate this 'balance' and wonder how this newly disturbed situation or relationship is going to affect me. What am I going to have to give up? And what will the consequences be for me and for my relationships with others? These questions occur in all relationships - friendships, marriages, partnerships, at school, in work and in politics.

Sometimes, people (or groups) are never able to compromise. They are determined to get their way every time. They can never see themselves as ever not being in the right; they make sure that in any conflict, the other is always in the wrong. Or it may be at work, the levels of reward and recognition may make you feel ignored or under-valued. How do you manage those feelings and address those situations maturely?

In your parents' unhappy marriage and acrimonious divorce, their self-interest trumped all feelings of regard for the other. Harsh principles of habit and behaviour destroyed their individual capacities for loving, or more likely, frustrated their need to receive love from the other. The absence of compromise and consideration of the other led to the destruction of everything that they had hoped to acquire in their marriage - home, children, a family, status and recognition - happiness! Isn't it amazing, and so incredibly sad, that two people's search for love, became so dominated by their feelings of frustration, disappointment and hatred for each other in their struggle for individual recognition that they sacrificed the joint venture upon which they had originally embarked? This strange drive towards destruction (and death) goes by the name of Thanatos, and human beings have struggled against it from the beginning of human history through the development of art, music, justice, laws and positive social living. But from time to time, Thanatos breaks through and the collapse of relationships and of kindness and collaboration, occurs through envy and hatred, and may lead to war, both between individuals, as in the case of your parents, or between nations, as between Russia and Ukraine, between Israelis and Palestinians, and between Christians and Jews. Eros and Thanatos are two sides of the same coin, and one must be careful about which side is up and active at any given moment.

This is a situation often seen at work in which people work together in harmony and creatively for ages producing good things together. And then suddenly, one party behaves selfishly, demands more than their fair share, takes credit for what both had achieved together, and then acts on those feelings by withdrawing from, or betraying the other. The flipside of their creativity then emerges - suddenly remembering previous long-forgotten insults to their dignity, and behaving in hurtful, spiteful ways towards other people in the present. In this way, relationships can be easily damaged or broken which are sometimes hard or impossible to repair.

Your studies in literature, drama and theatre have helped you gain a deep understanding of human drives – this shows in your work on the stage in modern-day versions of the great playwrights of the 19th and 20th Centuries. You have made connections between the characters in your plays and your own life. You have directed theatre exceedingly well, and this has helped you to reduce the degree of unhappiness that results from your parents' unhappiness. Learning is a journey, not a once-and-for-all achievement. You are travelling on this journey wisely, and despite the occasional dip into depression and despair, you are taking mature steps in both giving love and being able to receive it. Your dreams speak of your feelings of self-doubt and your ambitions to achieve a state of calm and tolerance of yourself. As your 3-year-old cousin, Sinai, cautioned me the other day, "life is a struggle". You are doing well in yours and you will come out a full and rounded individual with your own standards and values.

I expect you sometimes think about how you are going to sustain your relationships with your parents, as there will be times when you will want to be more with one than the other. You will want to be fair to them both, but you may also find it impossible to relate to them equally, because you will have different feelings towards and about each of them. One parent was exceptionally restrictive with you and the other was tolerant and understanding of your needs, providing softer opportunities for joy, togetherness, and laughter. Trust your feelings and do not feel guilty because you do not feel scrupulously fair in allocating your time to them. It is natural to get on better with one parent than with the other. Your mother is stricter; your father is more relaxed and accepting. He has made excellent use of his resources to reflect on how he can love you better and make up as far as he is able to for not being able to protect you from your mother, and for not being able to help your mother give you what you needed from her. There are wide differences in their capabilities to understand and give love and to receive it.

My best wishes to you, as you move forward steadily along the path you have chosen.

Your loving grandfather, Mannie

Letter #45

Allergies

29th March 2022

Dear Hallel

Like you, I suffer from allergies, but not to the same extent as you do. I never had to carry an EpiPen around with me, like you do. My allergic reactions produce an itchy nose and frequent sneezing, while your allergic reactions included itchy, red and watering eyes, wheezing, chest tightness, swollen lips, tongue and eyes, and when your allergies were unbelievably bad, you had tummy pain, and sometimes vomiting and diarrhoea. Breathing difficulties can lead to a life-threatening allergic reaction.

The most common allergic reactions result from certain foods, animal fur, pollens, mould, dust mites, certain medications, insect stings, perfumes and household chemicals. A person's immune system produces substances called antibodies that identify an allergen as harmful, even though it is not. When you encounter an allergen, your immune system's reaction can inflame your skin, sinuses, airways or digestive system. Allergies vary in their severity and can range from minor irritation to anaphylaxis - a potentially life-threatening emergency which is why you carry an EpiPen. We cannot cure allergies, but treatments can help relieve allergy symptoms.

This description implies an inert, passive person, a victim influenced by events or things "out there" that trigger allergic reactions in your body, but there are times when internal feelings and emotions also play a part in allergic reactions. For example, a body which is under stress releases hormones and other chemicals, including histamine, the powerful chemical that leads to allergic symptoms. While stress does not cause allergies, it can make an allergic reaction worse by increasing the histamine in your blood stream. This introduces the idea of the interplay between your body and your environment and between your mind and your body. Recent studies have shown that lifestyle, stress or trauma can result in the weakening of the immune system (another term for defences), and therefore cause an increase in allergic reaction, and raise levels of anxiety and depression.

Children of parents in serious conflict with each other, and divorcing parents, are significantly at risk of developing allergic reactions. Another factor that adds to a child's stress is the absence of escape from warring parents and the fallout of their toxic relationship – the child feels trapped at home and faces the fear of an imminent collapse of their once-safe world. Children need two parents who work together in harmony to look after them and provide a safe environment. The child who witnesses arguments, hostility, and conflict between parents, wonders what will happen to them and what they must do to keep themselves safe. Allergic reactions are the responses of the body in the face of impending threats and dangers of abandonment, as if it is aware of the looming collapse, and it produces antibodies.

Now speaking of the immune system producing antibodies, I am thinking of another altogether different situation when your body produces antibodies - this time of an affirming and sustaining kind. Whenever two people talk to each other, each one produces antibodies. One kind of antibody makes you feel listened to and affirmed, loved and accepted. They give you a warm feeling in your stomach; you breath calmly and have an overall sense of contentment that the person you are speaking to is trustworthy, even loved, because they recognise and respect your needs as an individual. Putting it simply, you are confident that you have a place in their minds, even in their hearts. Then there is the other sort of conversation in which you feel small, stupid and unimportant, hurt and humiliated. This type of conversation is usually an angry one, full of demands and criticism and this conversation makes you feel guilty, misguided and at fault. Your immune system leaps into action and produces antibodies to warn you that you are in danger, and you need to either defend yourself or remove yourself from the situation. If the other person is more powerful than you, like a parent, teacher or officer, you may feel you have no options but to suppress your feelings and just pray that the exchange will stop. And if it does not stop and you cannot escape, the situation becomes doubly dangerous as your immune system keeps on producing more antibodies in a never-ending cycle of threat and defence, until you either get out or break down.

You have been fortunate to spend time at the Midrasha where you had wonderful, empathic teachers and counsellors with whom you could discuss your deepest and most intimate feelings and thoughts and from whom you learned positive life lessons, including discernment - evaluating whether things are good or threatening. Importantly, you have learned what gratitude is and how to express it constructively. You are kind and generous and you have a life force in you that is immensely praiseworthy. You are kind to others, as you are kind to yourself. But your autoimmune system is not "kind" to you because it has confused real threats with unreal ones. Talking professionally to someone who understands the relationship between the mind and the body has been immensely helpful to you in letting go of the baggage that your parents' unhappy marriage has bequeathed to you. Keep talking! It is a sure antidote to your allergies by helping you separate trust from threat.

Speaking of trust, I must mention your relationship with Eyal. You both seem particularly good for each other and happy in one another's company. He is a dedicated support to you, and he helps you work things out in the relationship sphere. He is caring and considerate and he no doubt looks to you in return for support when dealing with his own feelings about his parents' divorce. My best wishes to both of you.

I wish you well in the Army. I am sure your life experiences will stand you in good stead in your work in supporting soldiers from disturbed family backgrounds. It is excellent work that you are doing in healing your soldiers, and through them, healing yourself, and providing a much-needed service to the Army.

Your loving grandfather, Mannie

Letter #46

The Religious Life

2nd April 2022

Dear Nadav

You have chosen to lead a religious life, and intriguingly, you have also chosen to study English literature. No doubt you will be thinking about how you will make sense, even reconcile, the two different approaches to understanding life, ethics, values and obligations, alongside the powerful human creative drives described in the great English novels of the 18th, 19th and 20th Centuries. This combination of Torah learning, and secular learning will both challenge and reinforce your beliefs. Be open to such challenges; do not be afraid. Allow your mind to accept new thinking that is relevant to modern life, as much as our ancient traditions are. By being a bridge between Torah and Talmudic literature and contemporary stories, you will inspire young people to follow you, as you have amply demonstrated in your outstanding service as an officer in the Army. You have the potential to grow in wisdom and influence.

Nadav, let your Yeshiva studies and your English literature studies go together hand in hand. Integrate them. You will not regret it. Rav Lichtenstein was versed in both spheres and that counted in part for his greatness. Greatness will come to you too by navigating and helping others to navigate the rocky journey between living up to the ideals set for us by others and those that arise from deep within ourselves.

It may be hard for you to accept that your parents have not been able to provide a contented home that is your due. Their unhappy marriage and divorce have hurt you, but that should not prevent you finding happiness in your life. You should put out of your mind the awful pictures of their conflict and find in your life the calmness and stillness that enables you to discover your own thoughts and feelings; to find the strength to become your own person. I say this out of a deep love for you, and out of concern of what we may have contributed to producing the circumstances you now find yourself in. Divorce forces one to think about the past and about what we could have done differently, but it is also true that the past is another country and there is little chance of putting right now the behaviours of years ago. You must live with the fractures of your life; you should not feel responsible for events over which you do not have responsibility. You have huge strength of character, Nadav, a fine sense of humour, grit and determination, all necessary to help you overcome obstacles and find peace within yourself.

Nadav, bear in mind that all systems of belief can lose their essential messages and can turn into rigid dogmas or extreme fundamentalism. Human beings are not comfortable with uncertainty, and they will fill the gaps in their knowledge with untested ideas that often dwell in the realm of the unconscious mind. That is why science and literature urge us to evaluate our assumptions so that our ideas do not go down rabbit holes. One such example in today's world, is Vladimir Putin who so wishes to revive the former glory of Mother Russia and its imperialist past, that he is prepared to start World War III, and destroy nations and societies to fulfil his phantasy. You may call what he is doing a reasonable goal, as many people do, or you may call it madness. Managing to persuade the whole of Russian society, including the Russian Orthodox Church, may be a sign of good leadership, but he is also leading Russia towards its destruction to fulfil his dream of restoring a dead empire in an age when empires are over – in my view, that is not good values-based leadership.

It is the same with us, Nadav. As Jews, we aim to restore our heritage and traditions and to return to what we consider our former glory of Temple times. But, mostly, that is a myth; there was never a time that Israel was free from struggle and conflict with neighbouring empires. There was no pristine, paradise-like time, or if there was, it was short-lived. In my view, we have created an imaginary paradise as an ideal dream in our minds to compensate for the loss of our political autonomy and independence. Instead, we must ask ourselves how do we go forward? What kind of future do we want to create? And how do we get there? Remembering the past is important. I am thinking of the mitzva 'lizkor', to remember; there is no obligation to recreate the past. It is gone, and we must let it go. In my work as a psychotherapist and as a change consultant with organisations and societies, I have endeavoured to help people let go of redundant ideas and out-of-date rules and face a future for which new innovative ideas and approaches are necessary. The same is true for present-day Judaism and Zionism. You are the right person to help others bridge the gap between dreaming and reality and thereby lead people to living healthier and happier lives. Dredging up the ghosts of the past will not help you. Instead, offer hope of the future and what is achievable. The greatness of the Torah, in contrast to the futile saintliness at the heart of Christianity, describes our forebears as human beings in their greatness and in their imperfections. Having ideals is good, but idealisation offers nothing but tragedy. Torah defines their personalities in terms of their goodness (welcoming the stranger, loyalty and challenge), and in their weaknesses (jealousy, rivalry, impetuosity and cruelty). Even God is doubtful about what he has created and wishes He could undo what He has done, but He cannot. And so, it is with us mortals - we may be capable of dreaming of ascending to great heights and creating super, conflict-free societies, but the next day dawns and we wake up to the realities of our individual shortcomings and the limitations of our parents, other people and the world around us. The disappointment and the pain of what we cannot have, contributes to our growth and maturity and to an adult acceptance of what is possible.

I give you my blessings for a contented life, solid relationships and success in your endeavours.

Your loving grandfather, Mannie

Letter #47

Art

20th December 2022

Dear Elianna

You are six years old, and you are already showing a great interest and talent in drawing and painting. It is something you seem to want to do in every free moment you have. In fact, Grandma and I have two of your lovely drawings hanging on the wall in our house. Whenever we look at your drawings, we think of you and your interest in artistic expression.

This letter is meant to be an encouragement to you to continue finding satisfaction in producing beautiful drawings and paintings. You should find yourself a good, patient teacher to teach you the techniques and methods for producing good drawings and paintings. In addition to having the desire to put on paper, and later, on canvas, the images that you have in your mind, you also need the guidance of a teacher who has experience in art and who can teach you how to mix colours to create new colours, how to introduce depth, perspective, shape and light into your work.

You have a great gift, and you should develop it to your fullest potential.

There are several reasons why a person expresses themselves through art. Firstly, art is the production of symbols that have meaning, and meaning is what everyone strives to achieve in their lives. So, for example, a drawing of a flower is important for what it is – the representation of a flower - but it can also mean beauty, symmetry, Godliness, growth, development and a 'flowering' of something else, like love and affection; it might remind viewers of your paintings of a sweet smell that they remember from their childhood days. Art is an expression of symbols that connect us to important moments and people from our past.

It can be said, therefore, that artists are like messengers scurrying back and forth between our unconscious memories and the present time, evoking feelings of warmth, contentment and love. Of course, art can also remind us of things that we have lost, and a picture can make us feel sad and regretful. This is the greatness of art - it can touch people in many ways.

Secondly, art is the desire to make a mark on the world - to express what you see in the world in a slightly different way, and in this way give expression to the many different experiences that people have, which are based on their individual personalities, their family histories and their national and religious cultures. The artist may cover all these areas of human experience, or the artist may concentrate on one single object, like a flower.

Thirdly, art allows the artist and the viewer to be imaginative, to open their minds to different possibilities of thinking and seeing. Art is the wonderful opportunity to be in touch with the infinite because the artist is unafraid to think, to imagine and to act to produce something from inside themselves.

Elianna, like your name suggests "My God has answered", let your imagination flow onto the paper or canvas, as an expression of what is going on in your wonderfully creative mind, the beautiful pictures that you store there and want to share with the world.

Grandma and I take great pleasure in looking at your pictures in our house and we look forward to seeing many more of them.

Your loving grandfather, Mannie

Letter #48

A Letter to the Twins, Shiloh & Lily

21st February 2023

Dear Shiloh and Lily (4½)

We knew early on that your mummy was going to have twins, but what we did not know was how much joy you would bring into our lives - your loveliness, your playfulness, your eagerness for the stories your grandparents, Grandma and I, would tell you while you sat around on the grass and enjoying taking over the story and finishing it with your own tales. Your boisterous adventures made us recall our younger days when we had the energy to run around like you do. Twins are very interesting to observe - how they develop into people with their own individual personalities, while at the same time regarding themselves as closely aligned with each other, supporting one another in strange places. The whole idea of how twins grow into separate, but linked, people is fascinating.

Shiloh, you had a difficult start because the hospital staff felt you needed to be in an incubator for three days before being reunited with your mother, Lisa. Fortunately, your father, Yoram, knew how important the first hours and days of life are for bonding between mother and baby, and he stayed with you during those three days, holding you, stroking you, and soothing you with nice words and songs.

Lily, I recall the time when you looked at Shiloh lying next to you in your crib and you focused hard on him as if you were discovering for the first time that there was another person there next to you; you seemed to feel reassured that he was there as a familiar figure, someone who would continue to be part of you and your life.

As the weeks and months passed (you were living in our house at the time, until your mum and dad found a place of your own), you ate together in your highchairs in our kitchen, and you seem to feel that the amount of food that was placed before each of you was just right and fair. You noticed what the other was getting, and you did not protest or attempt to take the other's share. This cooperation extended into your play which you later called a 'team' and it was delightful watching you plan together, consult each other on what went where, and how you resolved your differences. Your teamwork was quite remarkable, and we noticed too, how the two of you would gang up against the adults, confuse them with your private language and plan deceptive strategies to defeat them. It was exhausting for your parents, and for us, but it was good to see you discovering your powers and how to do the things you wanted to do.

Shiloh, you have a keen interest in cars, in anything with wheels that moves. You build cars and work out what pieces go where - and you are not possessive - you willingly show me what you have done and even allow me to play with it for a bit. You are generous with your knowledge and understanding, explaining to me how the thing you have built works. You calculate height and distance, achieving the right balance of blocks that you are building – and, of course, your immense knowledge of dinosaurs, knowing the names of each type, the period of history in which they lived why they became extinct. You went looking for evidence of dinosaurs in our garden and got so very excited when you found a piece of old bone or a flint, happily reassuring Grandma that dinosaurs lived a long time ago during the Jurassic age and we should not worry.

Lily, your grace and beauty was simply wonderful to look at and when our eyes meet across the table, you make it clear that we have a special private connection, that involves no one else around the table - just you and me. Your movements are confident, you seem to feel grounded, knowing what you want and do not want. When the noise in the dining room gets too much for you, you take a book and read it under the table or in your private tent, coming out when you feel the room has quietened down. You also love your collection of fluffy toys which you seem to regard as your family which you feed with your toy food plates, knives and forks and cooker. You play for long periods on your own with "your family" talking kindly to them with great imagination and love.

Whenever grandma offers you a treat, you make sure to get some for Shiloh too. You have a beautiful way of thinking about others and showing concern, like the time you told grandma and me about your daddy's sore back. We could see that you were worried and that you wished that daddy would be better and healthy again soon.

Shiloh and Lily, in a few weeks you will be going to big school where you will be with different children than the children you know at nursery school. You will have different teachers, but it will also be exciting because you will learn new things and you are both very eager to learn new things, to understand the world you live in and to expand your relationships. You seem to fit in very smoothly to new situations and you make the most of your opportunities. Lily, on your last day at the nursery school concert, you spoke into the microphone when it was your turn, with confidence and seriousness. Your dancing was brilliant, in time to the music, and well-synchronised with your friends.

Shiloh, you were wonderful too, expressing what many people were feeling that the concert was too long, and it was time to end. You make your feelings known and you don't like being frustrated by the rules and demands that are sometimes imposed on you. Well done!

Dear Lily and Shiloh, I hope to write to you again in the way that you have called 'private conversations' whenever you visit us.

Your loving grandfather, Mannie

Letter #49

Nadav – Officer in the IDF and the Middle East War

9ᵗʰ December 2023

My Dearest Nadav

I write as an anxious grandfather to a beloved grandson who has put himself in the line of fire on behalf of his country and his people. Your commitment to the security of Israel, and through Israel, the rest of World Jewry, is solid and absolute, which, I am sure, keeps you going through these difficult times. I admire your brave leadership of the soldiers under your command – it is an inspiration.

You are also a man of peace who brings goodwill and cheer to others, always smiling and bringing a good message from the Almighty. I have seen evidence of the esteem and love that your soldiers have for you. There is no greater quality in leadership than the love that a leader has for the people they are leading. Nurture that love all your life, Nadav, which I know you will do through kindness, charity and words of Torah. You bring the qualities of human kindness and spiritual understanding into your personality, and they guide you in your relationships and in your behaviour in whatever role you are in.

I cannot imagine how terrifying some of your work in the army must be, but I'm also sure that you tackle your tasks with diligence, care, and tremendous skill. You are a team player which is obvious in the way you carry out your command as an "exceptional soldier". But there are other less visible aspects to your team membership - namely, that what you are doing, you are conscious of doing on behalf of others, too - on behalf of me, your parents, Adeena and Hallel, the State of Israel and on behalf of preserving humanity and justice for all freedom-loving people.

I salute you, Nadav, in doing this very difficult job, and I trust that you will come out of this war a stronger person, with a clear sense of the direction you wish to take in your life.

I offer you my blessings and may G-d go with you.

Your loving Grandfather, Mannie

Letter #50

Integration of Cultures

30th December 2023

Dear Kerem

From the first day you left home for school, you had to learn how to join groups and get used to the things that groups do. Your family was your first experience of a group, and you learned the different kinds of relationships in your family – (i) the relationship between your parents, Ollee and Danny, (ii) the relationship between your parents and your sisters, Matar, Elianna and Sinai, (iii) the different relationships between your sisters, and (iv) and the relationship between you and each of your sisters.

When you reach adolescence your group of friends will likely become more important to you than your family. And when later you get your first job, the group you will join, your work colleagues, your teammates, will assume another whole significance for you. Your football team is a very close group of players, and you know that you have to work together sharply to keep the ball away from the other team, and to score your goals. You will train hard with your team to win, and this may mean that sometimes you have to give up your wish to score, for example, by passing the ball to another member of your team, because he is in a better position to score. Teamwork can be very fulfilling, but also frustrating.

As you know, Kerem, through your mother, you are descended from a proud and illustrious Yemenite family who have close bonds with each other and with their extended families, and with the State of Israel, and by tradition look after one another with great care, love and warmth.

I had the pleasure several times of visiting your lovely grandparents, Ratzon and Ilana, in their family home in Herzliya and enjoying their hospitality. You are a joy to your family, and I notice that you are very special to Ratzon and Ilana. They admire you for your cleverness, your independence and your fun-loving attitude.

Amongst your many interests is playing the drums. I so enjoyed the videos of you playing the drums, your dad sent to us. Perhaps, other interests have replaced your interest in drums by now, but in whatever you choose to do, I know you will be enthusiastic, and you will give it your boundless energy.

Being the only boy in the family means that you have a special place in your dad's heart (and in mine!), but I imagine that at times it must be quite a struggle being the only boy among three sisters and especially having one, Matar, older than you. But I know that the two of you are also great friends and share things together, like the time Matar shared with you the story of my childhood, and the two of you, with a lot of care and concern, came to ask me if I was alright.

This shows you have great compassion for people and want only the best for them. You are also generous, Kerem, and curious to learn new things. You want to achieve much and sometimes the frustrations of not getting things just right can get the better of you. Do not let yourself be overcome with feelings of defeat, which I know from my own experience is the easiest thing to do. You are a person of enormous courage and perseverance. When you fall down, you pick yourself up and keep on running. So it is with the problems of schoolwork and of relationships. Keep your mind on making things work for you, while also holding on to your values of doing things well together with others. You are a great person to have around, and people enjoy your company. Keep it up, Kerem. I and your family, all of them, love you and all are rooting for you.

Your loving Grandfather, Mannie

Letter #51

Work Groups

30 December 2023

Dear Adeena

As you and I have been talking about 'work' lately, I thought I would write about my understanding of work and the way work is constructed and conducted, which includes, of course, the psychological bonding between colleagues which can be very close and personal as in, say, sports teams, actors in a play, fighting units in the military, or construction teams on a building site. Or the team can be held loosely together as in remote working when you may not see the person you are working with, or may be dependent on for your work, because they are in another country thousands of miles away.

At the Tavistock Institute, we have a long history of scientific research into the dynamics of groups, and, as you know, I have published extensively on the dynamics of systems, which includes both large human enterprises and small face-to-face groups. Our social scientists are interested in the influence such groups exert on both their individual members and on the organisations of which they form a part.

It is common to regard groups as being separate entities with purposes of their own, that are qualitatively different from the purposes of the individuals who make up the group. The focus on group characteristics in research has shown that productivity in groups rises when group members are given or take responsibility for the evaluation of their own work and the standards of the working group. There are different types of leaders of groups and different leadership styles, for instance, authoritarian leadership tends to weaken group morale and it has negative effects on the group's achievements. On the other hand, decisions made collectively by the group involving all its members tends to be more effective and efficient, even though it may take longer to achieve goals than authoritarian-led groups.

The Tavistock approach, developed at the Tavistock Institute of Human Relations since its inception in 1947, is a profound methodology for understanding and working with groups. It combines social psychiatry, psychoanalysis, and organizational behaviour to examine the unconscious processes within groups and how these dynamics affect both individual and the group's collective behaviour.

Key figures like Wilfred Bion, John Bowlby, and Eric Trist were instrumental in developing this approach. Bion's work on group dynamics, particularly his concept of "basic assumptions," forms a cornerstone of Tavistock thinking. Bion identified that groups often operate on unconscious assumptions, like dependency, fight-flight, or pairing modes, driven by underlying anxieties and defenses, which can undermine their primary task.

The Tavistock methodology is heavily influenced by psychoanalytic theories, particularly those of Sigmund Freud and Melanie Klein. Klein's ideas on object relations and the internal world of individuals provide a lens for understanding how personal histories and unconscious phantasies play out in group settings. These psychoanalytic roots allow practitioners to probe deeper than surface-level interactions, seeking to uncover the latent emotional currents that shape group behaviour.

Central to the Tavistock approach is the idea that groups function as complex systems with their own internal dynamics. The primary task is the explicit purpose of the group, such as completing a project or providing support. In contrast, basic assumptions refer to the unconscious, often irrational, behaviours that can divert the group from its primary task.

Another crucial concept is the "social defence system," a term coined by Isabel Menzies Lyth. This idea explains how groups develop collective defences to manage anxiety. For example, in a hospital setting, nurses might adopt rigid procedures and depersonalized interactions as a defense against the anxiety of dealing with illness and death. These defences, while providing short-term relief, can ultimately hinder effective functioning and innovation.

The Tavistock approach also emphasizes the importance of boundaries, authority, and role. Boundaries delineate the limits of the group's task, membership, and time frame. Authority involves the legitimate power to make decisions and enforce norms within the group. Role refers to the expected behaviours and responsibilities associated with a particular position within the group. Understanding these elements is crucial for diagnosing and addressing dysfunctions within the group.

The Tavistock approach has wide-ranging applications, from organizational consultancy to community development. In organizational settings, Tavistock-trained consultants often conduct group relations conferences, also known as the "Leicester conferences." These immersive events provide participants with the opportunity to explore their own behaviours and assumptions in real-time group settings. Through experiential learning, participants gain insights into the unconscious dynamics that influence their work and interactions.

In therapeutic communities and social care settings, the Tavistock approach is used to understand and address the collective dynamics that affect client care. By examining the social defence mechanisms and basic assumptions at play, practitioners can develop strategies to create more supportive and effective therapeutic environments.

The Tavistock methodology is also applied in educational settings to foster better learning environments. Educators and administrators trained in Tavistock principles can identify and address the unconscious factors that impede student engagement and institutional effectiveness. By working through these dynamics, schools can create more inclusive and responsive educational communities.

While the Tavistock approach offers deep insights into group dynamics, it is not without its critics. Some argue that its heavy reliance on psychoanalytic concepts can be abstract and difficult to operationalize in practical settings. Others point out that the focus on unconscious processes might overlook structural and systemic factors that also influence group behaviour.

However, the Tavistock approach's strength lies in its ability to illuminate the often-hidden emotional undercurrents that shape human interactions. By bringing these unconscious dynamics to the surface, the Tavistock methodology enables individuals and groups to gain greater self-awareness and agency. This awareness is particularly valuable in today's complex and rapidly changing organizational landscapes, where understanding the human element is crucial for achieving sustainable success.

The Tavistock approach to understanding and working with groups offers a rich, nuanced framework for exploring the unconscious processes that influence group behaviour. Despite its complexities and critics, the approach remains a vital resource for those seeking to foster healthier, more effective groups and organizations.

Your Loving Grandfather, Mannie

Letter #52

The Youngest Child

6th January 2024

Dear Sinai (4 years old)

You are the youngest of four children and I suppose sometimes it is easy to feel that you get lost in the crowd. But you have shown that no such thing happens to you. You are joyful and smiley, and you know how, in the nicest possible way, to get the attention you need. When you visit Grandma and me in London, or when we visit you in Jerusalem, I so much love it when you gently want to hold my hand, or to sit on my lap, or when you examine and ask questions about the bumps and scars on my face and hands. It is as if you are trying through the gentle art of touch to heal something that you think may be wrong with me. That kind of reaching out to people can be said to be "touching", that is, you 'touch' someone in their heart, and in turn, they 'touch' you in their heart and, in this way, an everlasting connection is made, a kind of reaching across the generations by making a bridge between grandparents and grandchildren. This kind of relationship helps us to know our places in life and in the world, the kind of warm human gestures that let us know who we are in the scheme of things, how we create our bearings of where we come from and where we are going to. And you do that touching so endearingly with a smile on your face and with a sweet affectionate softness in your voice and hands.

Because your mummy and daddy are sometimes busy, you have had to fend for yourself a lot and you have learned to be independent, finding things for yourself and busying yourself with your own games, reading a book or drawing pictures, or writing letters to Grandma and me.

I remember fondly when Grandma and I visited you, taking you to nursery in the morning and fetching you at lunchtime, walking back home and stopping to buy you an ice cream. You would talk to us about the things you did at nursery school, who your teachers were and the friends you played with. Everything you told us was spoken with such serious intensity. We listened closely to what you were saying - we were in very close private intimacy - no interruptions, no competition - just you and us. We enjoyed being with you so much. Naturally, when we are away from you, we miss you terribly and enjoy talking to you on WhatsApp.

Sinai, you go to big school now and you are learning new things. We are so sorry that we are not nearer to you to talk about your latest discoveries at school and how things are going with your friends. It is so interesting to hear you talk about them and what it all means for you. We cannot wait until the next time we meet you and continue our interesting conversations.

Of course, I must tell you that your cousins in London, Shiloh and Lily, love you and they often talk to us about the great times they had with you when you were here. They look at your photos on our walls and remember the times we had together. We hope your next visit will be soon.

Dear Sinai, you are naturally curious, and you want to find things out and to know more. You are not shy, and you ask many questions. It is so refreshing - you have an inquiring mind, as we see when each answer to your question is quickly followed by another question. My blessing to you is that you should remain ever curious, asking more and more questions - that is the best way of learning - you have an open mind, and you should do all you can to preserve that gift. You are a blessing to your parents who derive a lot of pleasure from you.

Your loving Grandfather, Mannie

Letter #53

Adeena's Birthday

11 February 2024

Good evening, Adeena,

We are here to celebrate the birthday of a wonderful person, charming, loving, thoughtful and a pioneer of new ideas and new challenges.

Tonight, people will celebrate your being, and your beauty, your intelligence and your personality in tributes, involving poetry, in memories, in videos and photographs that capture your essence from childhood through your adolescence and adulthood. I would like to share something about Adeena with everyone here tonight which came to me through a dream that I had last week in which Adeena appears and which tells us about her core wisdom and kindness.

Some background to the dream: I am a patient suffering from kidney failure and for the past two years I have been having kidney dialysis at the hospital three times a week. During this time, Leonie and I have been taught how to operate the dialyzing machine in preparation for moving from hospital treatment to home dialysis. Needless to say, this training takes up a huge part of our lives as we learn the intricacies of preparing the machine before the start of the dialysis, hooking up to the machine, watching out for any technical problems during the dialysis, and then finally coming off the machine at the end.

Now back to my dream. The time is during the middle part of the 20th century when the dialyzing technology was in its infancy. Today, the technology is hugely complex because the dialyzing machine has to perform about 7 or 8 functions, but in the dream, we were concerned with only four functions.

In the dream, I am charged with leading the 4 teams of engineers, chemists, physicists, technicians and doctors in designing and developing the machine. For this, I have selected about 20 to 25 people to investigate the requirements of each of the functions. The teams are due to report back on how they are going to develop and build the dialysing machine.

Adeena is the team leader of one of the teams and she takes her team of 5 or 6 people off to their workspace to do their investigations, which take several months, after which they will return to a gathering of all the teams to report on their findings and recommendations. The next part of the dream occurs several months later after the teams have completed their investigations. They are now assembled to present their reports to each other and the first stage in building the machine.

Adeena opens her address to the gathering: "In our investigations into how we can solve the problems of the task we have been given, we have had to conclude that in some fundamental sense, one of the solutions we would have to consider is the possibility that there is no solution"

Everyone is stunned by Adeena's remark. How can a problem not have a solution? There are murmurings of disagreement as everyone feels thrown out of their comfort zone and they're forced to consider Adeena's and her team's reflection that some problems may not have solutions.

As Chair of the gathering, I had to think quickly, and I realise that Adeena has just offered the gathering an earth-shattering perspective on the nature and meaning of life, on the mysteries of nature and the universe. Adeena and her team have challenged the teams to examine the all-too-human tendency to think in straight lines - that every dilemma must have an answer - that truth is not an object you can hold in your hand, but a moving target sometimes within sight and sometimes not.

Also in the dream, I continue to think about Adeena's theorem in relation to the familiar psychoanalytic concept of the "no-thing", because that is what Adeena appears to be offering us - that the "no-thing" is not 'nothing', that the "no-thing" is a thing that we are obliged to relate to, because unconsciously it dominates our everyday thoughts and actions, meaning that for every decision we make in our daily lives, there are other possible decisions that we have to abandon. This may sound simple - you cannot have your cake and eat it - but for many people the dilemma of the "no-thing" is a daily agony that can prevent them from getting on with their lives. The "no-thing" and its dominance in our lives is frustrating and a source of great destructiveness in the world - the Biblical Tohu Va'vohu (chaos) from which we have emerged is the Tohu Va'vohu to which we must return.

People do not like to hear these things, but dreams do sometimes reveal the stark truth about ourselves and the people who appear in them. Adeena, you have grappled with your "no-thing" from a young age with the maturity that was beyond your years in the way you addressed your own conflicts, and in the way, with brilliant clarity and kindness, you helped others around you to think about theirs.

There is a photograph of Adeena in our dining room which captures the spirit of the struggle with the "no-thing". The photograph is of Adeena taken by her father, Shanan, when she acted in the play by Nickolai Gogol called "The Marriage". In the photograph, Adeena is dressed in a flowing 19th Century gown, playing the part of Agafya Tichonovna who is looking pensive, worried and sad and the caption beneath the photograph reads: *"Oh dear! Oh dear! What a mess I am in. How will I ever make my choice? If only it involved one or two gentlemen... but there are four!!. It's so confusing. Thinking about it is making my head throb."*

Adeena, celebrating your birthday is a joy and an inspiration of a life fully lived in its many parts which you have knitted together in a uniquely integrated way. You are an inspiration to everyone who crosses your path. You are wise and compassionate, full of understanding and comprehension of our deep inexpressible selves. You pay a heavy price for this, but it also enlarges your universe and by generously sharing it with others, you help to enlarge theirs.

Happy Birthday Dearest Adeena. We are so sorry we cannot be with you, but we look forward in hope, to seeing you soon and giving you a big hug and a warm kiss.

Your loving Grandfather, Mannie

Letter #54

The Israel-Gaza War and Anti-Semitism

30th March 2023

My Dearest Adeena, Hallel & Eyal, Nadav, Matar, Kerem, Elianna, and Sinai

I find myself lost in thoughts of you, my precious grandchildren, living amidst the turmoil of the Israel-Gaza conflict. Each passing day weighs heavy with concern for your safety, both physical and emotional, as the unrest persists. Grandma's and my heart aches knowing that you must endure such harrowing experiences at your young age.

In the middle of these trying times, I am haunted by the spectre of rising anti-Semitism, not only in our homeland but across the globe. It pains me deeply to witness the resurgence of such hatred, fuelled by ignorance and prejudice.

As you navigate through these tumultuous waters, I can only imagine the many emotions you must be feeling. It is a stark reminder of the fragility of peace and the complexities of our world. The noise of conflicts, from Gaza to Ukraine, Taiwan to beyond, may leave you feeling adrift in a sea of uncertainty, questioning the world you are inheriting.

Yet, amidst the chaos, I urge you to hold steadfast to the values that define our heritage. Our shared history, steeped in resilience and faith, offers guidance in these turbulent times. Reflecting on the story of Avraham, our forefather who dared to challenge conventional beliefs, we find solace in the enduring power of conviction and compassion.

Avraham's journey, fraught with doubt and sacrifice, serves as a beacon of hope in the darkest of hours. His unwavering commitment to kindness, generosity, and peace echoes through the ages, a testament to the enduring legacy of our people.

My beloved grandchildren, in the face of adversity, I implore you to stand tall and proud, unwavering in your convictions. Let not the shadows of hatred dim the light of your spirit. Embrace the world with open hearts and minds, guided by the timeless values that define our faith.

Know that you are not alone in this journey. Across oceans and continents, your family stands united in love and solidarity. Together, we shall weather the storm, drawing strength from our shared heritage and the bonds that bind us as family.

With all my love and blessings,

Your devoted Grandfather, Mannie

Letter #55

The Impact of Kidney Dialysis on Me

8th June 2024

Dear Shanan, Yoram and Danny

I have had regular in-hospital kidney dialysis for the past 2¼ years during which time I was trained in the intricacies of self-administration as part of my preparation for doing dialysis at home. The move to home dialysis occurred in April this year, meaning that I have been dialyzing at home for about 6 weeks and I've had enough time to assess the changes to my life. For a start, I increased the frequency of dialyzing from three times a week to four; and reduced the amount of time of each session from 3¾ hours to 3¼ hours. An advantage of home dialysis is greater flexibility in the use of time. I have the choice of dialyzing in the morning, afternoon or evening, thus enabling me to offer appointments to patients or clients at different times. Very slowly, I am re-establishing my former work timetable and feeling much better for it.

But what about the physical, psychological and relationship aspects of the dialyzing? I would say these are profound and in the reviews I have with my home dialysis nurse and my nephrology consultant, I have talked about it, and I talk about the impact on me in greater depth with my psychoanalyst.

Overall, I have to accept that the dialysis will not restore me to my previous state of health; rather the dialysis serves mainly to slow down the rate of my deterioration, and I cannot escape the feeling that it is my death that is really being postponed. I feel it physically in the fatigue that overcomes me for about 24-36 hours after each dialyzing session, the need to sleep and other forms of withdrawal. I am losing weight and while I enjoy the compliments that I look good, younger and fitter, I am aware that I'm wasting away and soon there will be little left of me to give up. My skin is rough and scaly and in places it shrivels as the muscles waste away. There are other physical symptoms like the loss of appetite, sleep disturbances, and lack of interest in things that once interested me very much and which were sources of strong motivations. I'm acutely aware of changes in my emotional responses towards what was previously important to me, for example, new project work. My relationship with Leonie seems to be undergoing a change with more distance developing between us, complicated by the changes in my dependency on her. She is my carer now and I feel there is a reversal of our traditional relationship in which I was more often in the role of her carer. Leonie is not resentful, as she might be, at these changes, but she now has to pay more attention and think ahead about my needs - at a time when it is getting more difficult for her to function at full capacity due to her ageing and increasing infirmity. We both feel high levels of anxiety about one of us tipping over into greater helplessness. Balancing our states of need is precarious and I wonder how long our circumstances can carry on like this before one of us becomes fully incapacitated. Meanwhile, we are grateful for every day that we have together. We are grateful that we have the means to support ourselves at home and the regular, happy contact we have with our children and grandchildren (and soon our great grandchildren).

I worry about a diminishing ability to produce new ideas and thoughts. I like to think that I can bring fresh perspectives to my clinical, research and consultancy work, but sometimes I feel that my brain power is slowly disappearing, like the loss of blood that sometimes occurs when I am needling, like a feeling that I was allotted a fixed amount of blood and brain power and losing any of it will not be replaced. I talk about this a lot to my psychoanalyst and I'm hugely grateful for the opportunity of talking about my feelings with him because it is a rare place where death can be spoken about without fear of censure or being dismissed with false reassurance. My psychoanalyst noted recently that the dialyzing procedures seemed to satisfy an obsessional part of myself. At first, I did not understand what he meant, but later I recognised what he was getting at - that the demands of performing the steps necessary for dialyzing (60 steps coming on, and 30 steps coming off) that have to be carried out in the right sequence, are giving me a framework for completing an activity which makes me feel good when I get them right - a sense of accomplishment follows - like watching the picture emerge as the pieces of a jigsaw puzzle are put in place.

And then there is the miraculous side of the dialyzing process - plunging a needle into each of my artery and vein, connecting the needles to the bloodlines that transport almost all the blood in my body into the dialyzing machine where the toxins in my blood pass through a membrane and my blood returns in a more or less purified form into my body. And another key function is the removal of excess fluids in my body that my kidneys are no longer able to do.

Many supplies are needed to complete the dialyzing process - tanks of acid, needles, syringes, chemicals, filters, water softeners, gauze, tapes, plasters and more. Once a month, on cue the supplier company delivers all the necessary supplies, the cupboards are filled up again, and I'm ready to go off again for another month. I feel enormously grateful to the NHS that invests so much in me and keeps me alive. It could all be so different, and I sometimes wonder why "the other", i.e. letting kidney patients die, doesn't happen - after all, the patients that are kept alive are hardly productive citizens of society, so it must be a different set of values than economic ones that keep the system going. The other day, I was sitting in the Kidney Centre waiting room waiting for my appointment with my renal consultant, and I was observing the behaviour of the patients and receptionists sitting behind a glass screen. As a group, the patients are usually angry, cantankerous and impatient, demanding or complaining about long waits for their transport home and other requests. The interesting thing was that the receptionists never flustered or got angry back. They all responded to the patients' as cherished individuals, spoken to kindly and problems quickly resolved.

I imagine that the receptionists had been well-trained to control their emotions and to always put on a friendly face towards the patients. Something benevolent was going on, in spite of the frustrations and any negative feelings staff might be harbouring towards the patients. This is a side of the NHS one does not see in the critical reports about the state of the NHS in the media.

    Your loving Dad, Mannie

Letter #56

Decisions Made and Unmade

4th August 2024

Dear Shanan

Last weekend an incident occurred in the family that aroused strong unhappy feelings in everyone. You and I discussed the incident and its consequences, and we discovered that we have different views on its origins, its meaning and how the stress could have been avoided, and what we should do to repair the hiatus. Everyone involved in the incident, and even those who were only peripherally involved, has a view as to who was responsible for raising the temperature, but one thing was common – the feeling of "it was not me!" - and fingers were pointed towards someone else, as if to say, if that person had behaved differently, then we would not be in this mess.

It is tempting to point to someone else as the cause when problems arise – it simplifies the problem to have one individual who can be identified as the culprit because we can then place that individual in the dock, bring all the evidence to condemn that individual and everyone else gets off completely free from the responsibility and shame of hurting others, or penalty that might have to be paid. We all wish to escape feelings of shame and guilt for when things don't work out as we would have wished.

So let me outline what happened, as I understand it, and I would like to use Tavistock socio-technical frame of reference as an offer of a key to the conundrum.

Shanan, you had an idea which turned into a 'project'. You wanted to help me gain a better self-image following a significant weight loss that results from my dialysis treatment. I do not have many well-fitting clothes, mostly old shapeless clothes - you said that it is important to dress well in good fitting clothes and that would change how I feel.

At this point, Hallel offered an interesting theory and a practical solution to the problem of how to declutter systematically. Everything Hallel said made sense to me and matched my own wishes to tidy out my cupboards, and overcome my resistance to doing so, due to the lack of time and the bother, my physical tiredness, and the dust that gets me sniffing and sneezing.

So, the three of us arrived at a workable solution that had the hallmarks of ease, speed, convenience, plus the benefits of acquiring a new set of clothes and a new self-image. We set about going through each item of clothing, and before long we had filled three or four large plastic bags ready for collection by a charity. We had fun; we laughed at the ridiculous way I looked in clothes with sleeves down to my knees and wide trouser legs.

While all this was going on in my bedroom, Mum and Eyal were downstairs, not part of the process, except feeling marginalised, and Mum, especially, feeling that in all probability she would just have to fall in with other people's plans, whereas she had good ideas of her own on what we should do. For example, instead of going shopping the next day, which would have been your last day with us, she had suggested we should order clothes online, choose what we wanted and return the rest. This online option was rejected and Mum fell into line with the rest of us knowing from experience that I would not like the shopping expedition. She was surprised at my acquiescence, but I think we were all caught up in your enthusiasm for the project, and I was happy and willing to go along with it. We all admired the empty spaces in my wardrobe, and I looked forward to replacing the lost items with more fashionable clothes the next day.

Then, on Sunday morning, Yoram arrives at the house to drop Shiloh off, and when he heard about our plan, he persuasively expressed his reservations, reminding me and Mum of how much I dislike shopping, how I tire quickly, and he supported the idea of relying on online shopping. Yoram was convincing in his arguments, and I agreed with him that online shopping was preferable to spending an afternoon in stuffy changing cubicles.

Yoram and I then left for my gym session and when I returned home an hour later, I discovered there had been an almighty row in my absence between Mum, you and Hallel, about Yoram.

Since on second thoughts, it had been no trouble for me going along with you and Hallel to buy new clothes, I changed my mind again, and said I would go shopping with you as we had originally agreed. So, this whole palaver was due to me and my passivity in first agreeing with one option and then another and then back to the first option. The person you and Hallel should have been angry with was me, not Mum. And it occurs to me that there might be a simpler explanation for the family row, which is this: in my group relations work, I have learned that for groups to reach consensus on decisions, requires large amounts of patience and a deep respect for the group process. Conflicts, whether at the family level, or at the organisational and international levels, demands that people have a better understanding and respect for group process, viz., when a group makes a decision, the decision belongs to the group, and not to the individual who raised it originally. No individual has the right to unilaterally change it, not even the individual who originally piloted the decision, or the individual who is the focus of the decision. Decisions made by the group can only be amended or terminated by the group. Inevitably, when decisions are revoked unilaterally, conflict results, and feelings of exclusion and rejection are aroused, leading to dysfunctional behaviour, even to revolutions and war, in the case of international relations. Just look around you for the evidence of this self-evident truth.

I hope you will be able to accept this point of view together with my heartfelt apology for being so idiotically thoughtless in changing my mind several times without first consulting everyone who had participated in making the original decision, whether or not they were physically present in the original group. This is another lesson to consider – groups are made up of people in the room and the people who are not in the room! Who holds in mind the interests of the people not in the room?

The incident taught me the importance of inclusive decision-making and respect for group processes. Acknowledging our roles in the conflict, especially my own indecisiveness, is crucial for healing. I hope we can move forward with a deeper understanding and a commitment to better communication. My sincere apologies for any hurt caused, and I look forward to reconciling and strengthening our family bonds.

Your loving Dad, Mannie

Letter #57

A Letter to Leonie

3rd September 2024

Dear Leonie,

As I sit down to write this letter, I am filled with gratitude and a profound sense of wonder at the journey we have shared together. It is a journey marked by love, resilience, partnership, and the intertwining of two lives devoted to understanding the minds and hearts of others—yours in the vibrant classrooms and teacher training halls, and mine in the quiet, reflective space of the consulting room.

Reflecting on the years we have spent together, I am reminded of our early days—two young souls, filled with ambition and dreams, stepping into the unknown with little more than our love for each other and a shared commitment to building a life of purpose. We were young parents, grappling with the joys and anxieties of raising our children, Shanan, Yoram, and Danny, while navigating the uncertainties of emigration and the pressures of our evolving careers. I see now that it was in those early struggles, those sleepless nights and difficult decisions, that the foundations of our partnership were forged.

Your journey in education was not just a career—it was a calling. From your days as a primary school teacher, nurturing young minds with patience and warmth, to your remarkable 15 years as Director of a teacher training programme, where you trained over 250 student teachers in a spirit of generosity, compassion and high standards. Despite the iniquitous, inhuman, wrong-headed behaviour of your employers and the year of anguished legal proceedings, you upheld your principles and maintained the highest standards of teaching, ensuring that each trainee felt seen, supported, and inspired. This is your legacy—a legacy of excellence in teaching, achieved even in the face of adversity.

I have always admired your dedication, your tireless commitment to your students and trainees, and your unwavering belief in the transformative power of education. You saw beyond the child's mistakes to their potential, just as you saw beyond the trainee's nervousness to their promise. It is no exaggeration to say that you have left an indelible mark on countless lives.

And yet, even as you gave so much to your students and trainees, you were the heart of our family. You brought warmth, laughter, and a steadfast love that held us all together. In the most challenging times, when I was consumed by the intensity of my own work in psychotherapy—confronting the pain, confusion, and hidden sorrows of others—you were my anchor. You listened, comforted, and gently guided me back to myself when I seemed lost in the labyrinth of other people's stories.

In my own career, as I moved from social work to psychiatric social work, and ultimately to psychoanalytic psychotherapy and organisational and group relations consultancy, your support was unwavering. You encouraged me to follow my passion for understanding the depths of the human mind, even when it meant long hours, personal sacrifices, and the emotional toll that such work inevitably brings. It was you who helped me see that healing others required first confronting my own inner struggles, a journey I embarked on through my own psychoanalytic treatment.

Together, we navigated the delicate balance between our professional commitments and the needs of our children. We made mistakes, as all parents do. But we also learned, adapted, and grew together. I see in our children—now parents themselves—the values we tried to impart - compassion, integrity, resilience, and a deep respect for the life of the mind and the heart. These are values that we shared, taught, and lived.

I sometimes think of our shared interest in child development and the influence of the family on young minds, not just as a professional focus but as the very philosophy that shaped our own parenting. We understood that our words, actions, and even our silences would become part of our children's inner worlds, just as our own childhoods had shaped us. We tried to offer them the freedom to grow, while remaining a secure base to which they could always return.

Leonie, as I look back on our life together, I am overwhelmed by a sense of gratitude. You have been my partner, my confidant, my compass. Our love has been a steady flame, illuminating the darkest of times and warming the brightest. Even in moments of doubt and difficulty, we have always found our way back to each other, drawn together by a love that is both tender and enduring.

There is so much I could say, but perhaps it can be summed up in a single truth: My life has been immeasurably richer because of you. I have learned from you, leaned on you, laughed with you, and loved you with all my heart.

Yours always, Mannie

Conclusion

This is the concluding part of my memoir that is written in the form of letters to my children and grandchildren. At the time of writing, I am pleased to report that my family is expanding through the birth of a great-granddaughter, Nahar, to Hallel and Eyal and Nadav's marriage to Tamar. My Israeli family have gone through great trials during the past year of conflict between Israel and Hamas in Gaza. It is almost unbearable to think how the lives of two generations after me have got caught up in the gargantuan enmity between two peoples that has lasted a century and shows no signs of abating. Even exhaustion does not seem to lead the parties concerned to want to stop the destruction. And of course, it is a strange note on which to finish writing this book. It comes of the pessimism with which I have viewed the conflict, viz. that the players seem to be carrying the dynamics of peace and hatred permanently imprinted on their relationship and on each other's enduring belief that the conflict can only be resolved with the annihilation of the other. Accommodation seems impossible; the enmity is too strong; only short intervals of quiet exist between renewed bouts of aggression. The pious breast-beating of officials, politicians and journalists around the world seem of no consequence as the parties fight to the death. That seems like the parties to the conflict living under a life and death struggle that appears to be the lot of humankind – an existence that boils over into a ferocious struggle every now and again, and which gets readily projected into each other. In every conflict it is important to ask the question 'on whose behalf are the antagonists fighting each other?" because only then I believe is there the slightest chance of the conflict abating – when the spectators take back their fascination with the aggressive impulses of the fighting parties.

This message is not a positive one on which to end this book, especially as the conflict in the Middle East is not the only conflagration occurring right now. The fires seem to be spreading, and people are talking as if World War III has already begun. Talk of using nuclear weapons seems so glib as if the world is getting used to the idea of Armageddon and preparing to face oblivion. We can wonder at the pleadings of the past 80 years of "never again" and how easy it is for humankind to march deliberately and consciously towards a fiery end. This insane drive is without explanation - no wonder people believe in the untouchable Gods who are thought of as driving people wildly to their ends. What are the lessons we learn from this madness of "better dead than red" a slogan of the Cold War? Perhaps the drive of liberty and freedom is just as strong as the drive towards repression and slavery, and these two states of national thinking keep rotating every fifty to 100 years, like two rolling thunderclaps and electrical charges in the heavens. This is a terrible legacy to leave to one's descendants, I would prefer to leave a message of hope and the prospect of a peaceful harmonious future, but in the present state of affairs, this is a hard thing to do.

So, my message to my children and grandchildren is - be alert to destructive drives that stoke the fires of false pride and arrogance. Pay attention to your needs and to the needs of others and work in partnership with respect and love to achieve healthier patterns of belief and living. The earth, itself is a unitary living organism, can sustain only so much destruction before it spits everyone and everything out. Individuals are small, puny and relatively powerless, but by standing together in optimism, great things can be achieved.

As I write these concluding words, my granddaughter, Matar Emily Sher, daughter to Danny and Ollie Menachem-Sher, is getting ready to celebrate her Bat Mitzvah, her coming of age. She is bright, intelligent, caring and beautiful and excited about passing into adulthood, willingly facing the burdens of responsibility that come with it. As I write, WhatsApps are coming through on my phone with photographs of the preparations for Matar's Bat Mitzvah celebration tonight. Matar, you look so beautiful, serious and grown up and it makes me joyful to think that life carries on in the spirit of sharing, support and confidence. May you be guided by the presence of so much love of your family and friends who express that wonderful ideal of connected lives of nurturance and reciprocal support.

A testimonial from Adeena Sher, Granddaughter

Reading *Timeless Lessons* felt like being invited into a deeply personal and profoundly courageous inner world — where my grandfather navigates love, loss, identity, and the slow letting-go of life with extraordinary honesty and grace.

As his granddaughter, I was moved by his openness, and grateful for the opportunity to witness his reflections on life, aging, and family. The book became a living dialogue between generations — a space where his voice and mine could meet across time, experience, and perspective.

As I read on, I realized how deeply his writing echoed what I've been learning in my psychodrama training — the emotional layers of separation, endings, and the therapeutic space between people.

But before anything else, my experience of this book was personal. It was about love, legacy, and the rare intimacy of watching someone you care for reflect on life, and begin — gently, consciously — to say goodbye.

— **Adeena Sher, granddaughter and psychodrama student**